Housing America's Workforce

Case Studies and Lessons from the Experts

About the Urban Land Institute

The Urban Land Institute is a nonprofit research and education organization whose mission is to provide leadership in the responsible use of land and in creating and sustaining thriving communities worldwide.

The Institute maintains a membership representing a broad spectrum of interests and sponsors a wide variety of educational programs and forums to encourage an open exchange of ideas and sharing of experience. ULI initiates research that anticipates emerging land use trends and issues, provides advisory services, and publishes a wide variety of materials to disseminate information on land use development.

Established in 1936, the Institute today has nearly 30,000 members and associates from some 92 countries, representing the entire spectrum of the land use and development disciplines. Professionals represented include developers, builders, property owners, investors, architects, public officials, planners, real estate brokers, appraisers, attorneys, engineers, financiers, academics, students, and librarians.

ULI relies heavily on the experience of its members. It is through member involvement and information resources that ULI has been able to set standards of excellence in development practice. The Institute is recognized internationally as one of America's most respected and widely quoted sources of objective information on urban planning, growth, and development.

Recommended bibliographic listing:

Urban Land Institute. *Housing America's Workforce: Case Studies and Lessons from the Experts.* Washington, D.C.: Urban Land Institute, 2012.

ISBN: 978-0-87420-203-8

Project Staff

Lynn Ross
Executive Director, ULI Terwilliger Center
for Housing

Gayle Berens
Senior Vice President, Education and
Advisory Group

Sandra Robles
Research Director, ULI Terwilliger Center
for Housing

Adrienne Schmitz
Senior Director, Publications

Daniel Lobo
Manager, Awards and Publications

James Mulligan
Managing Editor

Joanne Platt, Publications
Professionals LLC
Manuscript Editor

Betsy VanBuskirk
Creative Director

Deanna Pineda
Muse Advertising Design
Cover Design and Layout

Craig Chapman
Senior Director, Publishing Operations

InterCommunicationsInc®
Book Design

Authors

Richard Rosan
President, ULI Foundation

Christina Rosan
Assistant Professor and Director of
Environmental Studies, Department
of Geography and Urban Studies,
Temple University

Lynn Ross
Executive Director, ULI Terwilliger Center
for Housing

Sandra Robles
Research Director, ULI Terwilliger Center
for Housing

Adrienne Schmitz
Senior Director, Publications

Theodore Thoerig
Manager, Awards and Publications

About the Jack Kemp Award

ULI's Jack Kemp Workforce Housing Models of Excellence Award recognizes exemplary developments that meet workforce housing needs in high-cost communities and honors developers that demonstrate leadership and creativity in providing expanded housing opportunities for America's working families.

The awards jury, composed of the ULI Terwilliger Center for Housing's National Advisory Board, evaluates developments based on the following criteria:

- Affordability;
- Proximity to centers of employment and transportation hubs;
- Quality of the design and site planning;
- Involvement of public and private partnerships;
- Use of regulatory reform to reduce costs;
- Energy efficiency;
- Sustainable green construction and land development;
- Innovative building technologies and systems; and
- Replicability of the development.

Established in 2008, the awards program was renamed by the Terwilliger Center's National Advisory Board in honor of former secretary of housing and urban development Jack Kemp for his tireless efforts to improve affordable housing opportunities for America's working families. The late Secretary Kemp, who served on the Terwilliger Center National Advisory Board, was the author of the federal Enterprise Zones legislation to encourage entrepreneurship and job creation in urban America that continues to advocate the expansion of homeownership among the poor through resident management and ownership of public and subsidized housing.

About J. Ronald Terwilliger

J. Ronald Terwilliger is chairman emeritus of Trammell Crow Residential, which he joined in 1979. Trammell Crow Residential is a national residential real estate company and was the largest developer of multifamily housing in the United States during Terwilliger's tenure as CEO. He is past chairman of the Urban Land Institute and remains a trustee. Additionally, he is chairman emeritus of the Wharton Real Estate Center, past chairman of the Atlanta Neighborhood Development Partnership, and chairman of the board of directors for the I Have a Dream Foundation. Terwilliger is the immediate past chairman of the international board of directors of Habitat for Humanity, is an ex officio member of the board, and chairs Habitat's $4 billion Global Capital Campaign.

An honor graduate of the U.S. Naval Academy, Terwilliger served five years in the Navy. He received his MBA with High Distinction from the Harvard Graduate School of Business, where he was elected a Baker Scholar. Terwilliger is a past chairman of the National Association of Home Builders Multifamily Leadership Board.

Philanthropically, Terwilliger made a $5 million gift in 2007 to establish the ULI Terwilliger Center for Housing, where he serves as chairman of the Center's National Advisory Board. Terwilliger is chairman of the Enterprise Community Partners Board of Trustees and vice chairman of the Enterprise Community Investment Board of Directors. His $5 million gift to Enterprise to create the Enterprise Terwilliger Fund is expected to create 2,000 affordable homes annually. Terwilliger also served as chairman of the board for Habitat for Humanity International, where his $100 million legacy gift will help 60,000 families access improved housing conditions.

Terwilliger has been recognized with the ULI Atlanta Community Achievement Award and the ORT Award, bestowed for his support and efforts to improve the world through his good deeds. He received the Hearthstone Builder Humanity Award in 2006 for his commitment to housing-related charities and in 2008 was elected to the National Association of Home Builders Hall of Fame in recognition of his efforts to advance housing opportunities for all Americans.

In 2009, Terwilliger was honored by the National Housing Conference with the Person of the Year Award for his commitment and contributions to the affordable housing community. In addition, he has been honored by the U.S. Naval Academy with a 2009 Distinguished Graduate Award for his lifetime commitment to service, his personal character, and his distinguished contributions to our nation. In 2012, Terwilliger was honored with the National Patriotism Award by the National Foundation of Patriotism.

Partnership Strategies

Collaboration is an essential element in workforce housing. Partnership models between nonprofit and for-profit, educators and developers, and the public and private sectors highlight the broad variety of solutions that successful initiatives generate.

PROJECTS

Casa del Maestro, Phase II
Miller's Court
Renaissance Square
Woods Corner

"[W]e know your residents and we're going to build them high-quality housing."

—**Bruce Dorfman**

Casa del Maestro, Phase II

Santa Clara, California

The 70-unit Casa del Maestro is tucked into a 1950s-era suburban neighborhood containing single-family and low-rise multifamily dwellings, within walking distance or a short bike ride to over a dozen school campuses, a neighborhood retail center, and a grocery store.

PROJECT DATA

Developer
Education Housing Partners LLC
Mill Valley, California
www.thompsondorfman.com/edhousing.cfm

Public Partners
Santa Clara Unified School District
Santa Clara Redevelopment Agency

Design Architect
KTGY Group Inc.
Irvine, California
www.ktgy.com

Housing Information
Rental workforce units: 30

Occupancy Rate of Workforce Units: 100%

Project Affordability
Rental price: $950–$1,600

Area Median Income, 2011–2012
60% $62,160
100% $103,600
120% $124,320

Development Cost
$6,455,000

Development Timeline
Date acquired: May 2008
Date started: May 2008
Date opened: April 2009
Date completed: April 2009

In 2000, the Santa Clara Unified School District (SCUSD) faced an employee-retention crisis: in the previous five years, teacher attrition had increased by 300 percent. Faced with untenable turnover, the school district conducted a study that revealed that staff members who are able to live and work in the same community are more likely to remain long-term employees. As a result, the SCUSD engaged an unusual partner—the for-profit apartment developer Thompson|Dorfman Partners—to help create Casa del Maestro, a 70-unit rental housing project, as a tool for recruiting and retaining teachers, as well as a means to help them ultimately attain homeownership.

This unlikely partnership has yielded significant results: the attrition rate for young teachers in the school district has been less than 25 percent of that for similar teachers who do not receive this benefit, and approximately one-quarter of residents of the first phase have gone on to buy a home in the district through the mortgage assistance program.

Casa del Maestro, Phase II, represents the final 30 units of the rental develop-ment, all of which are situated on a 3.5-acre school district surplus site. The entire project is affordable to district teachers earning 60 percent of the U.S. Department of Housing and Urban Development program income limits for Santa Clara County.

THE PROBLEM
Located in the heart of Silicon Valley, Santa Clara is home to Intel, Sun Microsystems, Agilent Technologies, and many other high-tech companies, as well as Santa Clara University. With a population of 100,000 and a median household income of $103,600,

Santa Clara has become increasingly unaffordable for the teachers who work in the school district and earn between $34,000 and $63,000 annually. In high-cost areas like Santa Clara, employers must be innovative in recruiting and retaining the best employees, especially for public positions that are vital to the community.

Thus, the SCUSD must recruit a highly skilled and educated staff at a pay scale that starts at a much lower point than the area median household income. Moreover, turnover-related costs, including training, exceed $60,000 per new employee—money that the district cannot afford to spend.

THE PARTNERSHIP
In 2000, the SCUSD partnered with Thompson|Dorfman Partners LLC. The for-profit luxury apartment developer formed Education Housing Partners (EHP) to provide a high-quality turnkey project for the district. This collaboration leveraged the strengths of each partner to reduce overall development costs: the school district brought surplus land and unique finance structuring to the deal; the apartment builder provided the technical expertise and capacity. EHP began the first phase of Casa del Maestro in 2002. The result—the first teacher housing development in California that was built, owned, and operated by a public school district—was an overwhelming success: after an initial lottery for eligible teachers, the project has maintained a long waiting list. The second and final phase was completed in 2009.

Apartments are available only to teachers who have been in the school district fewer than three years. Units are leased at rents that are approximately 60

percent of current market rents, allowing teachers the opportunity to start saving the equity required to purchase a home. To encourage turnover and homeownership, teachers can live at Casa del Maestro for only up to five years, at which time they can access the school district's mortgage assistance program.

THE SOLUTION
To maximize the affordability of the units, the school district structured an innovative tax-exempt financing instrument, which also allowed the project to be built and operated at no cost to taxpayers and without ongoing subsidy. The district capitalized 87 percent of the $6.5 million cost for Phase II through certificates of participation, which allow school districts to finance capital improvement projects with little or no impact on the district's finances or bonding authority, and with favorable interest rates. Since payment and financing terms are structured and the school district is technically not taking on debt, public referenda are not required. In exchange for this contribution, the developers committed to a 30 percent setaside requirement at low-income levels for a period of 55 years.

Using a portion of a district-owned surplus school site for the project meant that there was no land cost for the development. The developer estimated that the land cost at the time of the construction of Phase II would have been about $1.5 to $2 million per acre. Since the district already owned the land, it could reduce municipal fees and eliminate school fees and property taxes. The developer, project consultants, school district, and jurisdiction worked together to reduce the costs of project development. As

an example, development fees were about 4 percent of the total budget, as opposed to the typical 8 percent fee structure for projects of this size. Overall soft costs were about 50 percent of customary totals.

THE PRODUCT

Casa del Maestro consists of three residential buildings and a recreation building, all with Victorian styling. Hip roofs create covered patios on the street side, while the rear of each unit faces open greens. Apartment layouts are varied, upscale, and comparable to most newly built luxury apartments in the Silicon Valley. All units have large floor plans, modern kitchens, air conditioning, decks or patios, and private garages (50 percent of which have direct access to a unit). The recreation building, which includes the community room, also anchors an attractively landscaped central common.

The development of Casa del Maestro, Phase II, incorporated numerous design and construction upgrades to improve environmental sustainability in order to meet LEED Silver guidelines, including a site plan that maximized solar exposure for units; lower parking ratios and reduced footprint to provide more open space; and energy standards that are 15 percent more efficient than those mandated by the state.

CONCLUSION

EHP has gone on to complete two projects in San Mateo County based on the Casa del Maestro model, validating the creative partnership between the public school district and a well-regarded apartment developer. "Even with a softening residential market, home prices and rental rates are still well beyond what most starting teachers can

afford in metropolitan areas in California, so this type of workforce housing is as vital as ever," said Bruce Dorfman, cofounder of Thompson|Dorfman Partners LLC. Casa del Maestro, which has remained fully leased and maintained a long waiting list, can serve as a model for not only other public school districts but also for public and private employers throughout the country.

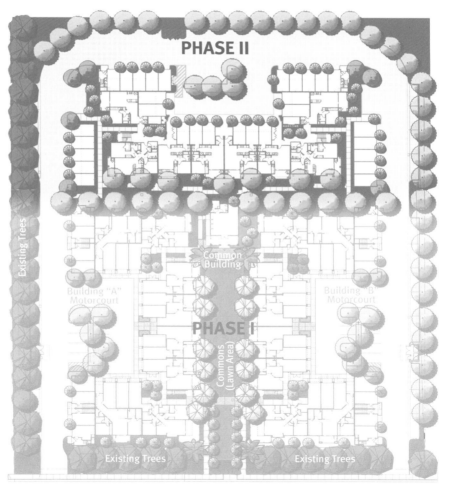

Lessons from Industry Leaders

Bruce Dorfman, Principal
Thompson | Dorfman Partners LLC
Santa Clara, California

RICHARD ROSAN: Why did the school district decide to build homes for teachers?

BRUCE DORFMAN: With the dot-com boom in the Silicon Valley in the late 1990s, we had such an increase in the workforce that it was putting huge pressure on rents and on home prices. Teachers were being hired at the Santa Clara Unified School District, which was one of the larger school districts in the Bay Area, with close to 20,000 students. New teachers were offered $40,000–$45,000. But they didn't realize that within a couple of years, they wouldn't be able to cover rent with that money; and, as a matter of fact, rents more than doubled in a five-year period.

ROSAN: What was the school district's response?

DORFMAN: The school district started to see an alarming increase in its attrition rate. I believe it increased to 300 percent during that same period. And then the superintendent started doing some demographic analysis, and he realized that he had a lot of young, new teachers and he had a lot of older teachers, but he didn't have a lot of teachers making the transition from young to old. The older teachers were unique in that they owned homes generally within the district so they could afford to live there. The younger teachers were effectively being priced out of the market.

ROSAN: What policies did the school district adopt to create housing opportunities for teachers?

DORFMAN: They initiated a two-prong approach. The first was a mortgage assistance program and the second was a teacher housing scheme—something to help recruit and retain teachers in the district. Ultimately, the school district decided it needed to put its toe in the water; initially, it was going to develop 40 units. It had a surplus school site, which was about 25–30 acres, two acres of which it was going to use for the project.

ROSAN: What was the quality of the units you developed?

DORFMAN: We developed a product that frankly is somewhat nicer from a product standpoint than what we would be doing for market rate just by virtue of our being able to build at lower density; consequently, all the units have attached garage parking, most with direct access. And we're building 20 units per acre. But the school district put 40 units on the table, a $6 million budget, and two acres. It owned the land, so the land was free. And it also didn't include the financing costs because it capitalized the financing internally.

ROSAN: Were you surprised that the school district chose your firm, a for-profit developer?

DORFMAN: We went through an RFQ [request for quotation] process. Interestingly, at the school district's initial informational session, we sat down with about eight other firms, all of which were nonprofits. The nonprofits were looking at it much differently than we were. They were looking at bringing their financing sources (tax credits, tax-exempt bonds, and so forth). The school district didn't need that and our pitch was "we know your residents and we're going to build them high-quality housing, and we're going to do it on a turnkey basis for them." We got a small development fee for the project and had our costs reimbursed.

ROSAN: Was there a strict design review process?

DORFMAN: We had internal design review. But I would say that we were probably more focused on the design than the city was for the very reason that we appreciated that this project could become a model. For the sake of its being reproducible for other communities, it's got to be a pretty nice place.

ROSAN: How did the financing work?

DORFMAN: The school district capitalized the $6.5 million by issuing certificates of participation. What was interesting about the certificates of participation was (1) they didn't require approval of the electorate and (2) they didn't have any requirements for affordability. So there were no strings on it—such as 40 percent of the units had to be leased to people making 60 percent of the median. Ironically, most of these teachers made too much so they wouldn't qualify for those units. That's the problem with some of the financing instruments for workforce housing.

ROSAN: And so with the $6.5 million, the district was able to carry this debt that it got with these kinds of rents?

DORFMAN: The rents at the time were somewhere in the range of $1–$1.10 per square foot, which was less than one-half the market.

ROSAN: So it's about $1,000 for a two-bedroom apartment?

DORFMAN: They started off at under $700 for a one-bedroom unit. And as we were nearing construction, the school district opened up a lottery system to teachers who had been in the district for over three years. The district received over 100 inquiries for 40 units. Consequently, it held this lottery. It was a big event, and we drew 75 names. The majority of them—one through 45—selected a home and signed up.

ROSAN: Does the $1.10 per square foot cover all operating costs? No subsidy is going into it?

DORFMAN: No. The bottom line was no subsidies. Operating costs covered an operating reserve and it covered the debt service.

ROSAN: Was there some rule for how long a teacher could stay there?

DORFMAN: Teachers could stay there for five years, and the whole hope was that during that five-year period they could put away a little nest egg that they could roll into the homeownership program.

ROSAN: What percentage of the teachers live in these developments?

DORFMAN: With the additional units from Casa del Maestro, Phase II, 10 percent of the 700 teachers in the district live there. I think what's really compelling is how many teachers have lived there and then moved into the mortgage assistance program.

"We took a look at the average starting salary of a teacher in Baltimore. . . . Then, we worked backward from that number to make it work."

—Evan H. Morville

Miller's Court

Baltimore, Maryland

Built in 1874 as the manufacturing site for the American Can Company, Miller's Court has experienced a renaissance as a mixed-use building with 40 workforce rental units targeted toward teachers and 30,000 square feet of ground-floor office space with reduced rent for educational nonprofits serving Baltimore's public schools.

PROJECT DATA

Developer
Seawall Development Company
Baltimore, Maryland
www.seawalldevelopment.com

Public Partners
City of Baltimore
State of Maryland

Design Architect
Marks, Thomas Architects
Baltimore, Maryland
www.marks-thomas.com

Housing Information
Total number of units: 40
Workforce rental units: 40

Occupancy Rate of Workforce Units: 100%

Project Affordability
Rental price: $700–$1,500

Area Median Income, 2011–2012
60% $50,700
100% $84,500
120% $101,400

Development Cost
$22 million

Development Timeline
Date acquired: July 2007
Date started: May 2008
Date rentals opened: July 2009
Date completed: August 2009

Case Study | Miller's Court
Baltimore, Maryland

Located in historic Charles Village, the conversion of the American Can Company factory building into a multipurpose educational life center includes one-, two-, and three-bedroom apartments ranging from $700 to $1,500 a month for teachers who have recently moved to Baltimore through teacher recruitment services. The LEED-NC Gold project represents a significant housing tool that can sustain the continuity and energy of local school staff, critical components for improving the Baltimore public school system.

THE PROBLEM

For years, the Baltimore public school system was regarded as one of the country's worst. In addition to low graduation rates, slumping enrollment, and low proficiency levels, the system also had trouble recruiting and retaining teachers. Those teachers who were recruited, often through the Teach for America program, arrived with little time to get settled and little assistance in locating safe, affordable housing. Absent a support structure, teachers can experience isolation and become overwhelmed by living alone in a new city. These issues can cause educators to resign their positions early, compounding retention problems in an already-troubled school system. Miller's Court was designed to provide a housing solution for this problem.

In addition to the city-wide issue of teacher retention, Miller's Court also aims to repair a hole in the local neighborhood fabric. For 63 years, the squat building on the northwest corner of Howard and 26th Streets in Baltimore's Remington neighborhood housed the H.F. Miller Tin Can and Box Manufacturing Company. When it closed its doors in 1953, the vacancy erased an important employer and activity generator in the local community, a void from which the community had yet to truly recover.

THE SOLUTION

The goal of Miller's Court is to make the housing transition easier for new teachers coming into Baltimore. The development was designed explicitly to build a sense of community among the residents, providing the support system so critically needed by these new teachers. A broader goal of the developers is to craft a positive experience and impression of Baltimore for these educators, so that after their contract expires they might continue to live and teach in the city, improving the stability of the school system and Baltimore's middle class.

Seawall Development Company had ten current teachers serve as a focus group, helping the development and design team understand what amenities were important to this unique group of residents. The result was a mixed-use building, which features both community

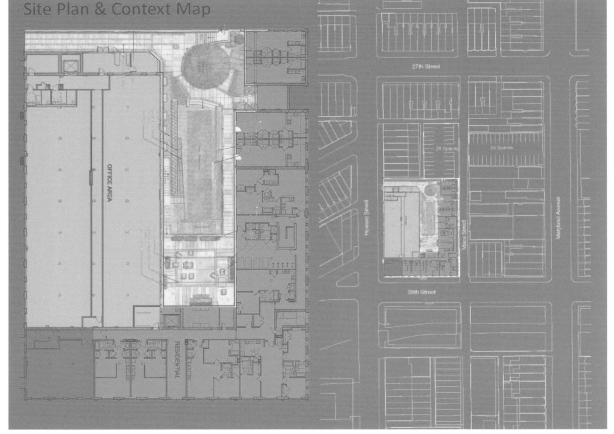

Site Plan & Context Map

space and education-oriented office space along with a mix of apartments.

Another outcome of the focus group was the reprioritization of certain elements of the design; for instance, the creation of an on-site copy room with significantly discounted rates, greatly reducing the amount of time and money teachers spend preparing materials—hidden costs that are often forgotten outside education circles. Also, the inclusion of a bathroom for each bedroom—two-bedroom apartments have two bathrooms, for example—made it more attractive for teachers looking to room together to cut costs. Perhaps the most important amenity, however, is the sense of community and camaraderie that is created in a residential setting composed entirely of devoted and energetic teachers.

FINANCING

The developer used a broad array of tax-assisted financing to reduce the amount of debt used, and ultimately to reduce the rental prices of the apartments. Of the $22 million development cost, approximately $12 million was financed through the sale of a mix of federal and state tax credits, with about $8 million covered by a traditional loan. The most significant of these financing tools was the combination of federal New Markets Tax Credits with federal and state historic preservation tax credits, which covered 55 percent of the total project cost. Additionally, the developer lined up very low interest loans from the city of Baltimore and the state of Maryland, adding $1.5 million in below-market-rate funds. Lastly, the developer deferred a large part of the development fee to reduce the amount of senior debt needed to finance the project.

On the operations side, the developer was able to secure Enterprise Zone Tax Credits, Brownfields Tax Credits, and local historic preservation tax incentives that essentially froze the project's real estate taxes at predevelopment levels for ten years, thus saving hundreds of thousands of dollars per year in operating expenses.

THE PRODUCT

The Miller's Court mixed-use program consists of one-, two-, and three-bedroom apartments targeted at teachers new to Baltimore through teacher-recruiting programs, coupled with office and conference space targeted at nonprofit organizations that support the school system and Baltimore youth. The one-bedroom units rent for between $700 and $850; the two-bedroom units for $1,200 to $1,400, and the three-bedroom units for $1,500. Each apartment features dark bamboo floors, 12- to 14-foot-high wood-beamed ceilings, exposed brick interior walls, and large windows.

The renovation of Miller's Court achieved LEED-NC Gold certification. In addition to the more common sustainable elements, such as low-flow toilets, motion-sensing lights, and Energy Star appliances, the developer installed an innovative mechanical system that combined the cooling tower and boiler systems in the commercial space with the residential units. The higher-efficiency and centralized system reduced energy consumption in the residential units and also eliminated the need to place 40 individual compressor/condensers on site.

CONCLUSION

Miller's Court is a sustainable workforce housing model that has had both a

micro impact—filling the void of an abandoned manufacturing facility—and a macro impact—creating a housing tool to attract and retain teachers in the beleaguered Baltimore school system. The project has been an overwhelming success: it has been 100 percent leased since the day it opened its doors and currently has a waiting list of more than 200 teachers.

This development concept is not a one-off project with a unique or finite funding source. The funding mechanisms used to create workforce housing at Miller's Court are readily accessible in any city with older buildings and census tracts that qualify for New Markets Tax Credits. In fact, the developer is using the same model at Union Mill, a similar renovation project that will combine office space for nonprofits with workforce housing for Baltimore teachers.

Lessons from Industry Leaders

Evan H. Morville, Developer
Seawall Development Company
Baltimore, Maryland

RICHARD ROSAN: What was the driving force behind this project?

EVAN MORVILLE: We don't look at ourselves as real estate developers but as social entrepreneurs. How can we use real estate to effect social change? And in this case, it was in education. So at Miller's Court, we wanted to develop a project that would allow us to market to a specific target—in this case, teachers—who we felt were underserved in the city of Baltimore.

In the school system here, there are about 25 different education nonprofits throughout the city—25 different locations, 25 different landlords, 25 different rents, no appreciation of scale, efficiency, or collaboration. We wanted to find a way to bring those groups together in one place. Also, on the other side, we recognized that the city was hiring anywhere from 700 to 1,000 new teachers each year. The biggest problem for Baltimore schools was retaining teachers.

ROSAN: So how did you put these ideas into practice?

MORVILLE: We started to look at different buildings. About three years ago, we found Miller's Court and quickly realized that we could marry the two ideas: you could have housing for teachers that would help with retention and attraction, and you could give them the support they needed with office space for education nonprofits.

ROSAN: Explain the office component of this project.

MORVILLE: We have 30,000 square feet of office space for nonprofits serving the education system. Today, we have ten nonprofits that employ around

100 people. Through the use of New Markets Tax Credits, state and federal historic tax credits, and some soft loans from the state of Maryland and the city of Baltimore, we are able to offer them Class A space at a Class C price, $18 a square foot.

The real interesting part about the office side is that we stress that you only rent what you use. When these nonprofits were in the basement of the townhouse, they had a little conference room; they had a little bathroom; and they had a little kitchen. Well, how often do you really use all those things? Not that often. So here we offer shared space: a kitchenette, a 3,500-square-foot conference center, and restrooms. Those amenities aren't calculated in their rent on a square-footage basis. So whereas they were maybe renting 1,000-square-foot spaces, now they only pay for an 800-square-foot space. We are finding that most of the nonprofits are saving 20–30 percent a year on their annual rental expense.

ROSAN: Is it working? Is this whole idea of their being all together more useful?

MORVILLE: We knew that in theory there was a huge opportunity for collaboration—get a bunch of like-minded nonprofits. But it has taken off in a way that I don't think anyone of us is prepared for. We kind of call it "hallway cross-pollination." None of the nonprofits have merged . . . yet. But they are collaborating on projects. They are starting to combine efforts on grants and to improve their buying power on certain things.

ROSAN: The residential component—how did you make it work?

MORVILLE: We used a focus group of teachers to tell us what they wanted, how much they wanted to pay, and how they wanted to come together. We took a look at the average starting salary of a teacher in Baltimore, which is $42,000 a year. What rent did they want to pay? Then, we worked backward from that

number to make it work. To get there, we used what we call the perfect storm of financing: New Markets Tax Credits.

To access the New Markets Tax Credit, you have to mix uses—office and housing in this case—since it's not just for housing . . . which was perfect in our case, since it worked with the overall mission.

ROSAN: What other financial tools did you use?

MORVILLE: The building cost was $2.3 million. The entire development cost was $20 million. Approximately $12 million of the cost was financed through tax-credit equity. In addition to New Markets Tax Credits, we used federal and state historic tax credits. The remaining $8 million is traditional debt.

ROSAN: So this mix of tax credits created an environment where you were able to pull the price of these apartments down to the price points that worked for teachers?

MORVILLE: Exactly, by increasing our tax-credit equity and by reducing our debt, we were able to reduce our monthly mortgage payment to a level that would allow us to reduce the expense of the apartment. We have one-bedrooms that rent for $750—that's with the teacher discount—where the market rate on that would probably be $1,100.

ROSAN: You don't do any market rate?

MORVILLE: Because of fair housing laws, anybody can live in this building who wants to. But they are pretty expensive at market rate. If you are a full-time teacher, you get the discount. But if somebody else comes in and says I want an apartment, he or she would have to pay the market-rate price.

ROSAN: What do you think is your main competition?

MORVILLE: Baltimore rowhouses. Teachers can all group up and live in a rowhouse, absolutely. But they are not

going to have free parking. And they'd have to pay utilities, and they'd have to share a bathroom. Through our focus groups, we found that people wanted a bathroom and a bedroom. So our two-bedroom units have two bathrooms, which make the whole roommate thing much more attractive. They also have a 24-hour fitness center, a copy center, a café, and a lounge.

What they also don't have living elsewhere is a community. Our residents constitute a huge support system, with like-minded individuals. And that is our abstract amenity. Ninety-five percent of the people said in their exit interviews that the thing they love most about living at Miller's Court is the support system: you know, having an awesome day and coming home and being able to pass Joe Shmoe in the hallway and say, "You are never going to believe what happened"; or having a terrible day and having people to vent to. And it's amazing how it works.

ROSAN: What has the project done for the surrounding neighborhood?

MORVILLE: There is so much more street activity. There is a restaurant right up on the corner called Sweet Sin, which probably would've gone out of business. A new restaurant is opening; a coffee shop opened on the corner. And then from a residential standpoint, this building sat vacant for 20 years. It was boarded up, not to mention dangerous. Now it's the opposite.

Another broader impact is one we hope to see. As you know, these teachers are not going to be living in our building forever. What we would love to see is for somebody to move from the Midwest, spend two years in Baltimore, spend a year or two in Miller's Court, and have a wonderful first impression of the city and want to stay and start a family in Baltimore. That's the big goal.

"The house is designed to be as energy efficient as we can make it, and it's low maintenance—a lot of low-maintenance materials."

—JoAnn Copes

Renaissance Square

Baltimore, Maryland

Renaissance Square is a 17-acre, 115-unit residential development offering 65 workforce housing units in the Essex–Middle River community of Baltimore County, Maryland.

PROJECT DATA

Developers
Enterprise Homes Inc.
Baltimore, Maryland
www.enterprisecommunity.com

Mark Building Company
Owings Mills, Maryland
www.markbuilding.com

Public Partners
Baltimore County
U.S. Department of Housing and Urban Development

Design Architect
Shannon Comer Architects
Stevenson, Maryland
www.comerarchitects.com

Landscape Architect
Human and Rohde
Baltimore, Maryland
www.humanandrohde.com

Master Planner
Hord Coplan Macht
Baltimore, Maryland
www.hcm2.com

Housing Information
Workforce units: 65
Market-rate units: 50

Occupancy Rate of Workforce Units:
31 are complete and occupied with another eight under contract

Project Affordability
Workforce units: $224,375–$300,000
Units other than workforce: $280,000–$350,000

Area Median Income, 2011–2012
60% $50,700
100% $84,500
120% $101,400

Development Cost
$27,472,973

Development Timeline
Date acquired: January 2009
Date started: January 2009
Date opened: April 2009
Date completed: Scheduled for December 2013

Located in the Essex–Middle River community in Baltimore County, Maryland, Renaissance Square is a high-density, 17-acre residential development that offers 115 units in a mix of housing types; 65 of the units are reserved for households earning between 60 and 115 percent of the area median income (AMI). The development is about a quarter mile from the Baltimore Beltway (I-695), which connects to Interstate 95, and is about two miles from a MARC commuter rail stop. The area is centrally located to major job centers, including Aberdeen to the north in Harford County, home of the U.S. Army's Aberdeen Proving Ground, and Fort Meade to the south in Anne Arundel County. The site is located within a Baltimore County–designated Community Conservation Area—an aggressive program that establishes priority funding for distressed, older neighborhoods—and was previously home to a dilapidated housing complex consisting of over 300 units.

Baltimore County was first to initiate the site's redevelopment through an

informed series of planning charrettes, involving the Essex–Middle River community. After a bottom-up planning process, the county awarded the demolition and redevelopment of the blighted site to the joint venture of Enterprise Homes Inc. and the Mark Building Company in 2009.

THE PROBLEM

Renaissance Square sits on land that was formerly occupied by a dilapidated, functionally obsolete multifamily housing complex called the Kingsley Park Apartments. The complex—hastily constructed to house factory workers during World War II—fell into decline several years following the war. The apartments experienced high vacancy rates and, subsequently, had the highest number of police calls in the entire county. Despite Essex–Middle River's proximity to the employment hub of Baltimore City, decades of haphazard development had led to sprawl, rising crime rates, and a lack of quality housing for the county's workforce.

Community members had opposed previous revitalization efforts, fearing that developing additional income-restricted housing would lead to more crime and would exacerbate problems in a community that was already home to a disproportionate number of affordable units. During the 1990s, residents also objected to proposals for developing market-rate housing—fearing loss of property through eminent domain and an influx of tourists and chain stores.

In 2004, through a negotiated settlement with the former owner of the Kingsley Park Apartments, the U.S. Department of Housing and Urban Development (HUD) acquired the property and conveyed it to Baltimore County with deed restrictions that

required any new housing development to serve a mix of income groups.

THE SOLUTION

Once in title, the county relocated the remaining residents and eventually razed the former apartment complex to make way for new development. Simultaneously, the Baltimore County Council approved legislation that allowed latitude in development requirements when a development plan is created through a community-involved planning process known as the Renaissance Redevelopment Pilot Program. The intent of the pilot program was to facilitate "smart growth" redevelopment. Developers initiate the process by submitting a proposal to the county for a mixed-use, pedestrian-friendly project. If approved, the developer is assigned a professional charrette facilitator to engage community stakeholders in the design process. By hiring a professional urban design team to lead planning sessions with the community, the county ensured community support for the new development before applications for development approvals were submitted. The result of the planning sessions was a pattern book illustrating the desired site layout and housing types and the specific goals for creating a mixed-income, inter-generational community.

After a competitive public offering, the joint venture of Enterprise Homes Inc. and the Mark Building Company was selected as the master developer for the site. The Enterprise/Mark Building Joint Venture worked hand in hand with the county to ensure a product that was true to the vision and standards established by the pattern book. When the project was ready for permit applications, it received an expedited review, resulting in approved development plans and a new recorded plat within a nine-month time frame—about six months shorter than for a conventional project.

Adhering to the pattern book, 65 units are reserved for households in six specific income categories ranging from 60 to 115 percent of AMI. The county donated the land and contributed $4,131,000 to cover the cost of infrastructure and to ensure that the homes were priced at affordable rates. As the units are sold, the funds are reused to provide buyers with forgivable, silent second mortgages. If a unit is resold within five years, all proceeds of the second mortgage are returned to the county. If a unit is resold between six and 15 years, the buyer can recover equity up to 10 percent per year. Purchase prices range from $224,375 to $350,000, with second-mortgage financing of between $120,000 for the lowest-income buyers and $58,000 for higher-income households.

THE PRODUCT

The homes in Renaissance Square are situated within a 17-acre site and include 115 new homes—48 townhouses offered in two sizes and 67 detached homes in three designs and sizes. An 81-unit seniors' apartment building has also been developed on the site by Enterprise Homes Inc. The homes are designed in patterns commonly seen in high-density residential developments, with minimum rear and side setback requirements. Garages are primarily detached and are serviced by private alleys to the rear of the property. Public sidewalks connect the development to other neighboring communities, encouraging pedestrian traffic and helping the neighborhood blend with the surrounding community. The homes are designed with large front porches to encourage socialization and neighborliness. Because the development has a higher density than what would normally be allowed, the developers met open-

RENAISSANCE SQUARE
A COMMUNITY BY THE ENTERPRISE/MARK BUILDING COMPANY JOINT VENTURE

ILLUSTRATIVE PLAN

HUMAN & ROHDE, INC.
LANDSCAPE ARCHITECTS

space requirements due to a county-led effort to create an adjacent park.

Committed to meeting the Enterprise Green Communities design and development criteria, the developers go beyond addressing energy efficiency by just the use of Energy Star appliances. They also include GreenGuard building wrap and added attic insulation; paints, sealants, and adhesives with few volatile organic compounds (low-VOC); formaldehyde-free composite wood; carpet that meets the Green Label standard; windows with high-performance low-E glass; exhaust fans vented to the outside; and low-flow faucets, toilets, and shower heads. Exterior housing lights are triggered by sensors, and landscaping includes native species and drought-tolerant plants throughout the site. The overall green goal was to build a healthy environment, to conserve energy, and to minimize costs to owners and renters. With its high densities, front porches, and reduced automobile visibility, Renaissance Square has a walkable, urban feel that reduces sprawl and helps stabilize the Essex–Middle River community.

CONCLUSION

Renaissance Square resulted from the unique partnership of HUD, the county, the community, and the developer. The charrettes ensured community support for the vision and design of the project, thereby allowing the developer to proceed with an innovative master plan supported by both the county and the community. Renaissance Square replaced blight with high-quality, affordable options for moderate-income households seeking housing with easy access to public transportation in the established community of Essex–Middle River. Through a creative financing structure that puts moderate-income households in an integrated, walkable neighborhood proximate to their workplaces, this unique development addresses both affordability and sprawl.

Construction of the site began in 2009 and was followed by the first phase of development consisting of 35 for-sale homes. Completion of the entire community is expected by the end of 2013.

Lessons from Industry Leaders

Harvey Zieger, Senior Vice President
Enterprise Homes Inc.
Baltimore, Maryland

JoAnn Copes
Consultant with Copes Colvin Inc., Baltimore, Maryland, acting as development manager on behalf of Enterprise Homes Inc.

RICHARD ROSAN: Let's start at the beginning. This site was previously a World War II housing project that was in decline, with terrible crime. How did the city or the town get the U.S. Department of Housing and Urban Development to take it back?

JOANN COPES: I'm not sure about all of the details, but I know there was a long period of negotiation and HUD eventually took a deed in lieu of foreclosure from the owner.

ROSAN: And HUD agreed to put up the funds to tear it down?

COPES: No, the county did that out of its own funds. HUD took over the property and then conveyed it to the county while it was still occupied by tenants. And the county proceeded to provide counseling and relocation services to all the tenants.

ROSAN: So the county decided that it wanted a mixed-income community?

COPES: They decided to plan for this site through a community charrette process, which was a series of meetings led by a professional land use and architectural firm to try to develop an overall concept plan for the redevelopment. And so there was a lot of participation by people who lived in this area and other community stakeholders to make that determination. What they came up with was some multifamily housing for seniors surrounded by a for-sale community of both townhouses and single-family detached homes.

HARVEY ZIEGER: This Renaissance program or renaissance process was a very important program initiated by the previous Baltimore County Council, or Baltimore County Executive Jim Smith. It was the first development that was created under the Renaissance Redevelopment Pilot Program.

COPES: After they came up with their overall concept design, they developed a basic site plan and a pattern book, which detailed the kinds of housing and features that they wanted to see.

ROSAN: Did the pattern book have schematic designs for the housing?

COPES: Yes; it was done as part of the design process.

ZIEGER: With the input of the community.

ROSAN: So the layout that you now have is pretty much the layout that the county established?

COPES: It's very similar; they originally envisioned two seniors' buildings—in an L configuration—but there wasn't really enough room on site to do that. And it was too expensive to do two buildings versus one. We were selected through the RFP [request for proposal] process and then entered into more detailed negotiation. When HUD conveyed the land, it conveyed it with certain use restrictions relative to income to ensure that there would continue to be some affordable housing on this site. And so it mandated that a certain percentage of units be occupied by households earning under 80 percent of AMI and another percentage under 115 percent of AMI. Then the rest could be non-income-restricted; that was overall units, so that included the multifamily units. All

the multifamily units that we developed in the seniors' building served households under 60 percent of AMI. So that helped meet that requirement.

ROSAN: Do you own and operate the building?

COPES: Yes, through a limited partnership. Enterprise is the managing general partner.

ROSAN: They gave you the RFP, and did the county say that the land was going to be free?

COPES: No, they didn't say any of that; they just said they would give us a proposal. So we proposed that the land would have to be at no cost in order to meet the goals that they had set out, which required that even 20 of the for-sale units be restricted to households earning less than 80 percent of AMI. In order to meet those goals, we would need free land and a contribution of funds to defray the costs of the site development.

ROSAN: They agreed to how many dollars for site development?

COPES: $4,131,000.

ROSAN: Was that cash in or they did the work?

COPES: No, that's cash in on a reimbursement basis. So as we do the site development, we submit a draw like their lender and they fund the draw.

ROSAN: So there are two subsidies in here—one is the land, but the other is the whole infrastructure: roads, sewers, lighting, and so on?

COPES: The water, gas lines, stormwater

management, alleys . . . and in return for that cash, the amount of money that the buyers have to put up to buy the houses is much less than they actually cost to build because of the difference of the value of that subsidy. And that gets recorded at sale, as a soft second mortgage to the buyer that requires no payments.

ROSAN: Can you talk to me about a standard house? What would you sell that house for?

COPES: The standard house is targeted to a household earning between 80 and 90 percent of AMI. The sale price of that house would be $241,200; that's a house without a garage or a wraparound porch, but with a full porch across the front. The sales price of the house would be $241,200; the buyer would be required to get a mortgage of $178,305. The difference between that and the sales price is represented by this soft second mortgage of $80,770.

ZIEGER: And in that $80,770 is reflected the cost of the land and the infrastructure.

COPES: And the buyer's closing costs; the closing costs in Maryland tend to be very high, so we estimate the closing costs at $20,000. The buyers are putting down $2,500, and then we are defraying the difference between the purchase price and the first mortgage.

ROSAN: So the buyer only sees a $178,000-plus closing costs number in effect?

COPES: No, the buyer's contract says you are buying this house for $241,200. You are required to obtain a first mortgage of not less than $178,305, and we will provide an additional soft second financing of $60,395 toward the purchase price, and up to $20,380 for the closing price.

ROSAN: What happens to the soft mortgage?

COPES: The soft mortgage is in place for 15 years. For the first five years, it stays full; it does not reduce at all. If the buyers stay in the house, they don't pay anything. If they sell within the first five years, they owe that whole amount back to the county or it can be assumed by a subsequent buyer. But the buyer to whom they sell at any time in the first 15 years after they purchase the house has to fall within the same income target.

ROSAN: After 15 years, no money has been paid back on the second mortgage.

COPES: And the income restrictions and the equity restrictions have gone away.

ROSAN: But it is restricted. Let's say that after five years, I sell the house. Can I sell it for more than I paid for it?

COPES: There are equity restrictions; you can get up to 10 percent equity each year. The first year you can get 10 percent equity; the second year you can get 20 percent. But you are allowed to get back the equity that you created from paying down the mortgage.

ROSAN: The finishes seem to me to be really high quality. What did you do for energy savings?

COPES: Well, we meet all of the Enterprise Green Communities standards, and we also participate in the Baltimore Gas and Electric Company's Energy Star rebate program—all of our appliances are Energy Star. We have

upgraded insulation; we use cement backing for the bathrooms; and all the grout is sealed in the bathrooms. All the paints are low-VOC; all exhaust systems are vented to the outside. We have exterior lighting on sensors, so it comes on at dusk until dawn. All our light fixtures are Energy Star. All the lights you'll see use compact fluorescent bulbs. The house is designed to be as energy efficient as we can make it, and it's low maintenance—a lot of low-maintenance materials.

ZIEGER: It's to maintain the affordability.

ROSAN: What were your hard costs [bricks-and-mortar costs] for building a unit?

COPES: We are at about $80 per square foot; just for the bricks-and-sticks house. And you might not have noticed but parts of the county's pattern of requirements were things like all the townhouses have to have brick water tables around them. The foundation has to be brick clad on all sides. And so that pushes some of our costs up. The county required that a certain number of houses have porches, and they can't just be for show. They have to be eight-foot-deep porches. So there were various things in the pattern book they required; for example, a certain upgrade of siding because they wanted this to be presented as a high-quality, mixed-income community. So a lot of the upgraded features have been built into the price of our houses, which you wouldn't find in a standard house.

ROSAN: In terms of the public perception of what they are doing here; they have also stopped a major social problem.

COPES: They did, and created a high-quality community. The county has been focused on this general area for a long time, in trying to bring streetscaping. They put in a major regional park across the street, an extension of which is on our side of the street. And our house is in front. So the county has put a lot of focus on this area and has made major public investments.

ROSAN: So who are the clients?

COPES: Primarily first-time homebuyers. It's a mix of families and individuals, but primarily families and single moms. A lot of public employees have bought here.

ROSAN: Is there public transportation nearby?

COPES: The bus stop is right in front.

ROSAN: Do you think most residents commute downtown?

COPES: No, I think most of them probably work in the county and are going to Towson, or they are going to White Marsh. But there is also the MARC train; the station is not very far from here. So if you worked at Fort Meade or out in Aberdeen and you bought here, or you came in from the base realignment program, you can commute on the commuter line, or you can commute to D.C. on the commuter line. So it has a lot of advantages in terms of transportation and smart growth principles.

ZIEGER: And in the workforce units, you have police officers, teachers, government workers, and health care workers.

ROSAN: Now on the financing of the building, you mentioned tax credits.

committee, the project benefited from changes in local regulations to provide density bonuses for workforce housing; the allowance of multifamily affordable units in certain nonresidential zoning districts; and a waiver of building permit fees (saving approximately $35,200) and impact fees (saving approximately $53,000). The village also donated four lots to the MKCLT; the land trust then negotiated a contract for the adjacent six lots at market price ($950,000).

The MKCLT also employed modular construction methods at Woods Corner. Compared with concrete block construction, modular building reduced the cost of transporting building components. The MKCLT was able to design, construct, and transport each building on a total of four trucks. This method of construction and shipment helped the developer achieve a 66 percent reduction in shipping costs, a savings of $140,000. In addition, the MKCLT was able to negotiate a waiver of the sales tax typically charged to the general contractor by purchasing the units directly while maintaining the general contractor's liability for the unit and materials through the completion of construction. This savings was approximately $97,000.

The MKLCT secured a second mortgage construction loan from Monroe County, using the State Housing Initiatives Partnership (SHIP) Program in the amount of $315,000. On the sale of each unit, the MKCLT repaid SHIP approximately $19,600 per unit, and that amount was simultaneously lent to the homebuyers as downpayment assistance with no interest and no regular payments for 30 years. This subsidy can be transferred to future buyers during the 30-year period.

THE PRODUCT
The 1,360-square-foot townhouses, built by Bayview Homes, a local builder with extensive local experience, feature ten-foot ceilings and an open floor plan on the first floor along with front porches and rear decks outside. The homes have all been developed to meet the Florida Green Building Coalition's standards, featuring Energy Star–rated appliances and improved insulation. The units are built outside the floodplain and are constructed to withstand the dangers of hurricanes: all homes feature a 150-mile-per-hour hurricane wind load rating, impact-resistant glass on all second-story windows, and panel shutters on the first floor. These measures make the homes more easily insurable and ultimately lower maintenance costs, as well as improving resale potential.

The Florida Housing Coalition, a state-wide affordable housing nonprofit, of which the MKCLT is a member organization, provided technical assistance throughout the process. A licensed

general contractor acted as the owner's representative and provided construction supervision at no cost.

CONCLUSION
In a community where land is a precious commodity and growth controls are rigorous, Woods Corner provides an example of how strong partnerships and regulatory tools can help promote homeownership for the local workforce. The developer also had access to a creative array of cost-saving tactics through the local government. The community agreed to allow Woods Corner to bypass waiver fees, changed zoning laws to allow for a noncomplying use, donated a portion of the site, and provided downpayment assistance for prospective homebuyers. The developer also deployed modular construction techniques to save on construction and transportation costs and was ultimately able to pass along those savings to the homebuyer.

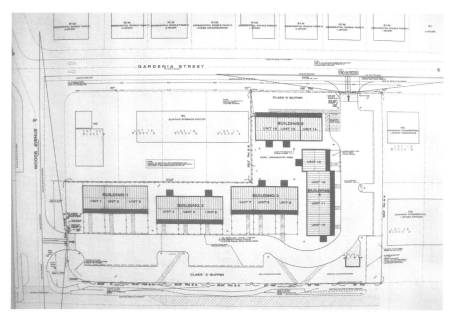

Lessons from Industry Leaders

Richard Casey Jr., Administrator
Middle Keys Community Land Trust Inc.
Marathon, Florida

Cheryl Culberson, Member of Local Planning Agency
Islamorada, Florida

RICHARD ROSAN: Why did you decide to develop this project?

RICHARD CASEY: In the Keys, it's difficult to find property for multifamily development because there are not many large buildable parcels remaining. We had an opportunity to combine two parcels: one that was a donation from the village of Islamorada (four lots) and the other we purchased with private financing (six lots). So that created a parcel that led to 16 units, which is one of the larger affordable housing developments in the entire county.

ROSAN: How does the density bonus work?

CASEY: All the local governments in the area give a density bonus for affordable/workforce housing. We ended up being able to build four additional units that we wouldn't have if it weren't affordable.

CHERYL CULBERSON: It was a change of policy. It took us two years to get the policy changed so that we could do this.

CASEY: My organization and the Workforce/Affordable Housing Citizens Advisory Committee of the village of Islamorada worked to make a number of changes in local ordinances to benefit more affordable development. In addition, the density bonus, one of the policy changes we made, was allowing affordable developments to be built on traditionally nonresidential parcels. The Woods Corner site was zoned highway commercial. Prior to just a couple of years ago, we would not have been able to build it. But again, due to the policy changes in the village, we were able to develop on a highway/commercial zone property.

ROSAN: Did you conceive of this project as for-sale housing from the beginning?

CASEY: Yes; as a community land trust, we are committed to homeownership. The community land trust model is a little different from traditional homeownership in that we lease you the underlying land for 99 years and then sell you the house (the improvement). Along with that lease, we have a resale price restriction that creates some long-term value to the community in resale-restrictive housing.

ROSAN: What is the restriction on the resale?

CASEY: You can resell it for 3 percent above the original sales price for every year that you live in the house. The homeowner gets to take the 3 percent out annually. The local governments are very committed to the land trust model, in that it balances the owner's ability to earn equity with the community's need for a permanent stock of affordable housing.

ROSAN: What were some of the public policy lessons?

CULBERSON: As the cost of land skyrocketed in 2003 and 2004, homes that were traditionally considered affordable were being snapped up, flipped, and sold for high costs. There was a loss of rental properties—due to conversions—and a subsequent demand for policy change. At the beginning, it was not so much about building homeownership as it was about protecting the rental property. But

no one was willing to build affordable housing that was restricted to rentals.

CASEY: From a policy standpoint, one of the things that made this project easier to do was that the village of Islamorada, recognizing the importance of affordable housing, has a standing affordable housing committee. So over the years, a group of citizens with affordable housing knowledge and familiarity has emerged. When we approached them—"Look this is what we'd like to do, but this is our problem"—the committee was happy to make recommendations to the city council. They helped us overcome some of those challenges.

ROSAN: The total cost for the units was $950,000. That's a pretty high number per unit.

CASEY: Just to put it in perspective, a single-family dry lot here at the time went for $120,000–$125,000. Again, we probably paid a premium, but it was an adjacent lot and four units turned into 16 lots. The construction costs were approximately $2.6 million. That's about $125 per square foot. When you add soft costs and interest expense, we're talking just about a $4 million project, or about $240,000 per unit. We sold the eight low-income units at $130,000 and the eight moderate-income units at $190,000. So there was a substantial subsidy—almost $110,000 for the low-income units and $55,000 for the workforce units. We worked it backward. If our target can afford $130,000 and $190,000, therefore we can borrow X amount. The rest is subsidy, and we know the construction costs, and where are we going to find the difference?

ROSAN: Despite the challenges you faced, do you think you accomplished your goals?

CASEY: Yes. I think in the end when you look at who is occupying the property, we certainly accomplished our goals. There are five teachers, two people in law enforcement, eight in the service industry—people that we need in our community. One of the questions we asked in our screening of owners was "How long have you lived in the community and how long have you worked in the community?" In our initial selection period—when we had an abundance of applicants—we took into account how long they'd lived here, how long they'd worked here, and whether they were active in the community in a nonprofit or volunteer role. We wanted to build something for the community. We thought that was important.

Financing and Regulatory Innovation

Often, developing workforce housing requires taking advantage of innovative regulatory tools or altogether approaching creative financing through methods and affordability controls. This approach manifests itself in several ways, including the use of land trusts, deployment of particularly innovative deed restrictions, or use of creative local or state policy custom-tailored for this purpose.

PROJECTS

33 Comm
Columbia Commons/Columbia Hicks Apartments
Fair Oaks Court
The Hayes at Railroad Square
The St. Aidan

"It really was a model process, and I attribute that to the public/private nature of the development."

—Susan Gittelman

33 Comm

Newton, Massachusetts

33 Comm is a mixed-income, 57-unit condominium development located in the Chestnut Hill community of Newton, Massachusetts, with 15 of its units reserved for working families.

PROJECT DATA

Developer
B'nai B'rith Housing New England
Brighton, Massachusetts
www.bbhousing.org

Public Partner
City of Newton, Massachusetts

Design Architect
Sheskey Architects
Quincy, Massachusetts
www.sheskeyarchitects.com

Landscape Architect
Stantec
Boston, Massachusetts
www.stantec.com

Housing Information
Market-rate condominiums: 42
Workforce condominiums: 15

Occupancy Rate of Workforce Units: 100%

Project Affordability
Purchase price for workforce units:
$138,000–$192,000

Area Median Income, 2011–2012
60% $54,960
100% $91,600
120% $109,920

Development Timeline
Date acquired: February 2007
Date started: March 2007
Date opened: February 2008
Date completed: June 2008

33 Comm is located in a pedestrian-friendly neighborhood adjacent to the Massachusetts Bay Transportation Authority's Boston College subway station, surrounded by neighborhood commercial establishments. The one- and two-bedroom condominiums are located across the street from Boston College—the city of Newton's second largest employer—and are easily accessible to job markets near downtown Boston. Nearby, a 71-acre public golf course and jogging trails surrounding the Cleveland Circle Reservoir serve to promote healthy living among residents.

33 Comm was developed by B'nai B'rith Housing New England, a professionally staffed, nonprofit organization dedicated to producing nonsectarian, affordable housing throughout Greater Boston.

THE PROBLEM

Although housing prices have declined to the pre–housing boom levels of the early 2000s, owner-occupied housing in Massachusetts is still less affordable than in many other parts of the United States. This dearth of affordable housing is especially true in the Chestnut Hill neighborhood of Newton—the nation's second-most-expensive college town (based on home prices). Newton lost much of its economic diversity and was grappling with how to retain young professionals who were priced out of the housing market; to resolve the issue, stakeholders turned to a statute that encourages affordable housing development.

Massachusetts law encourages the production of affordable housing in all cities and towns throughout the commonwealth. The law specifically targets households earning less than 80 percent of the area median income (AMI) for homeownership development. In rental development, the developer may designate 25 percent of total units to those earning less than 80 percent of AMI or may provide at least 20 percent of total units for low-income households (those earning less than 50 percent of AMI). The comprehensive permit statute, or 40B, was enacted to help address the statewide shortage of affordable housing by reducing barriers created by local approval processes, local zoning, and other restrictions. Chapter 40B allows local zoning boards to approve affordable housing development under flexible rules as long as at least 25 percent of the units have long-term affordability. Communities customarily provide a minimum of 10 percent of their housing inventory as affordable.

When 33 Comm was proposed, the city of Newton's affordable housing stock was only 7 percent of all housing. Also at that time, the city—home to 86,000 residents in 31,000 households—offered only 26 affordable homeownership units, significantly limiting homeownership opportunities for working families in the area. Upon the completion of 33 Comm—the first workforce housing development in the Chestnut Hill neighborhood of Newton—the project increased the overall affordable ownership stock in the city by more than 50 percent.

THE SOLUTION

The project was the result of an 18-month community/public review process. As part of this process, a "Friends" group was developed with over 200 members supporting the development. In addition, an unprecedented interfaith coalition consisting of over 30 local clergy and lay leaders was public in its support of the development.

The development received funding from local and state agencies. It received gap funding from the city of Newton's Community Preservation Act funds and a recoverable grant from the Massachusetts Affordable Housing Trust Fund to make it affordable to working families and compliant with Newton's community preservations goals. The project also involved a streamlined permitting process, due to its eligible 40B designation.

33 Comm promotes socioeconomic diversity by creating affordable housing in an upper-income neighborhood. The affordability of 33 Comm's 15 workforce units is secured by deed restrictions that designate them as permanently affordable to households at or below 80 percent of the area median income.

THE PRODUCT
In accordance with smart growth principles, 33 Comm used an existing building on its site. In addition, the project replaces a blighted single-family home with new higher-density housing. The new building is a four-story wood-frame structure built over a below-grade garage with 29 parking spaces. A surface lot provides additional parking. As an infill development within a well-established community, 33 Comm can use existing water, sewer, and other infrastructure. The property is an example of a transit-oriented development, as it increases the number of residents able to use the adjacent transit hub. In addition, its location promotes pedestrian activity with good sidewalks and street crossings—the infrastructure that must be present for walkability.

To promote sustainability at 33 Comm, native drought-resistant plants were used for landscaping, and rainwater runoff from the roof is being recharged into the groundwater. The project features Energy Star–rated appliances to reduce energy consumption. A cement fiber siding material is used for the building envelope that protects against air infiltration and requires less frequent care and repainting than wood products. During construction, the developers remediated a significant heating oil spill that occurred on the property, thereby repairing previous environmental damage to the site.

CONCLUSION
33 Comm is a beautifully designed and executed mixed-income development that integrates seamlessly into the surrounding community while offering high-quality housing at truly affordable prices. 33 Comm exemplifies how infill development can improve and serve a community, and the project's use of private/public partnerships shows promise for replication.

Lessons from Industry Leaders

Susan Gittelman, Executive Director
B'nai B'rith Housing New England
Brighton, Massachusetts

SANDRA ROBLES: Can you describe your organization?

SUSAN GITTELMAN: B'nai B'rith Housing New England is a not-for-profit organization whose mission is to ease the housing crisis by producing a steady stream of affordable housing throughout Greater Boston. Our housing is for individuals, young families, and elders, regardless of religion or background.

ROBLES: Can you describe the project?

GITTELMAN: The development is commonly known as 33 Comm, and it includes 57 units of mixed-income, condominium housing located in the Chestnut Hill community of Newton, Massachusetts. The development has two buildings: the Fairways, a newly constructed building with 44 units, and the Carriage House, a rehabbed building with 13 units.

ROBLES: How did you subsidize the workforce housing units?

GITTELMAN: The development received recoverable grant funding from local and state funding agencies. The city of Newton provided $1.2 million in gap funding from the Community Preservation Act funds to achieve project affordability and to satisfy other community preservation goals of the city. The Commonwealth of Massachusetts provided a $750,000 recoverable grant from its Affordable Housing Trust Fund to achieve project affordability. Based on the financial success of the project, the city and the commonwealth were each repaid approximately $300,000 of their own funds, consistent with the terms of such funding.

ROBLES: How are the workforce units incorporated into the development?

GITTELMAN: They are distributed throughout both buildings/phases. The Fairways building includes 11 workforce units and the Carriage House includes four workforce units.

ROBLES: Does your project have any unique sustainable features?

GITTELMAN: We applied a number of sustainable features to the development: native landscape plants that are drought resistant were used in landscaping; roof rainwater runoff is being recharged into the groundwater; the building envelope was sealed against air infiltration; and the project utilized Energy Star appliances. The materials for the exterior of the building were selected for durability and included cement siding that does not use wood products and requires less frequent care and repainting.

ROBLES: If you could pick one element, what was the key to making this project work?

GITTELMAN: I would say that our goal of creating cost efficiency was an important aspect to the project. In 2008 and 2009, there was a lot of volatility in the real estate market. Buyers were very value conscious, and we had planned for that in terms of keeping the unit layout very efficient (that is, 1,000-plus-square-foot units on average), and the buildings were well designed and appointed.

ROBLES: What would you do differently if you were to do it again?

GITTELMAN: I don't think we would do anything differently. It really was a model process, and I attribute that to the public/private nature of the development.

ROBLES: Any other comments about the project or the process, or advice on how this effort can be duplicated elsewhere?

GITTELMAN: We believe that this development is very replicable, particularly in affluent suburban communities that have lost much of their economic diversity and that are grappling with how to retain young professionals, families, and elders who want to return to these communities.

We have been told that the fact that the developer was a nonprofit is unusual (although not unique, I am sure). In some ways, I think the fact that we are a nonprofit actually helped us be successful because we were highly engaged and very accountable in our work.

"When we first took our idea to the different city agencies they said, 'This has never been done before.'"

—Tel Metzger

Columbia Commons/Columbia Hicks Apartments

New York, New York

Columbia Commons/Columbia Hicks consists of 95 workforce rental units and 42 homeownership units. The building is designed to reflect and enhance the character of the local neighborhood, which is a mixture of brownstone residential units.

PROJECT DATA

Developer
L&M Development Partners
Larchmont, New York
www.lmdevpartners.com

Public Partner
New York City Department of Housing
Preservation and Development
New York, New York

Design Architect
Gf55 Partners
New York, New York
www.gf55.com

Housing Information
Total number of units: 137
Workforce rental units: 95
Workforce for-sale units: 42

Occupancy Rate of Workforce Units: 100%

Project Affordability
Sales price: $399,000 (663 ft^2) to $935,000 (1,333 ft^2, three bedrooms)

Workforce Rental Units	Household Income
39	Less than 80% AMI
10	Less than 130% AMI
46	Less than 160% AMI

Area Median Income, 2011–2012

60%	$48,120
100%	$80,200
120%	$96,240

Development Cost
$51.6 million

Development Timeline

Date acquired:	September 2008
Date started:	November 2008
Date rentals/sales opened:	May 2011
Date completed:	December 2011

The Columbia Commons/Columbia Hicks Apartments project is a rare sight in the affluent Brooklyn neighborhood of Cobble Hill: a residential building that includes units affordable for moderate-income households. The project would have been impossible without a visionary scheme that allowed a commingling of funding sources that both mitigated risks for investors and ensured affordability for future residents.

THE PROBLEM

The Cobble Hill neighborhood of Brooklyn is an extremely desirable address with excellent transit access, one of the best schools in the city, and a limited, high-priced housing stock. Here, condominiums and co-ops routinely sell for more than $800,000 and townhouses sell for $1.5 to $4 million. Due in part to a local historic district, new multifamily construction is rare, and the opportunities for renters to live in the neighborhood at moderate rents and for purchasers to settle in at workforce-level prices are scarce. In addition, the developer faced public skepticism that affordable workforce housing could enhance an affluent urban neighborhood.

THE SOLUTION

At Columbia Commons/Columbia Hicks, affordability grew out of two areas: regulatory relief and creative financing. The project was built on an assemblage of roughly 50 percent public and 50 percent private land. The public land was rezoned from manufacturing (it was once the site of the Hamberger Christmas Display Factory) to residential, and the city sold it to L&M Development as a surplus property. The developer then merged the two properties and subdivided the resulting site into six separate condominiums—a complicated process that required a strong partnership with the New York City Department of Finance.

The financing combines taxable bonds, tax-credit equity, and a standard construction loan. For these sources to coexist in the same structure, lenders

required a condominium regime to be in place before construction to prevent the commingling of funds. For instance, two condominiums in the rental building are connected to two separate funding sources, so investors in one condominium are not subject to risk from the other. The New York City Department of Finance had never seen a condominium structure put in place before construction, but to achieve affordability, the department went forward with the creative plan.

The combination of for-sale and rental units also generated concern at Fannie Mae, which the developer used for end loan approval. L&M Development secured approval by carefully structuring the ownership; by designing a specialized approach to the mechanical, electrical, and plumbing systems; and by working with the insurance providers to issue a unique insurance policy. In the end, homebuyers were able to secure much more favorable interest rates through Fannie Mae.

THE PRODUCT
This large six-story project, which required rezoning because of height restrictions, provides both for-sale and rental units that are affordable to families at a range of income levels. Of the 95 rental units, 39 serve households making less than 80 percent of the area median income (AMI), ten serve those with incomes of up to 130 percent of AMI, and the remaining 46 are reserved for households with incomes of up to 160 percent of AMI. The 42 homeowner units are designed to be within conforming loans and to be affordable to first-time homebuyers, with one-bedroom units starting at $399,000.

The building design respects the surrounding community with its predominant building type: the brownstone. Exterior facades feature burnished brick and masonry elements, and interiors feature wide plank floors and farmhouse lighting. The exteriors of the rental and for-sale portions of the building are variegated, successfully mimicking the appearance of organic urban growth over time. This feature minimizes the "sore-thumb" monolithic appearance of many newly constructed large-scale buildings.

From construction methods to finish materials, the building is a model for sustainable design for workforce housing. The project includes dual-flush toilets and motion-controlled lighting as standard features. Highly efficient cavity wall insulation and roofs made of high-albedo materials add to energy efficiency.

CONCLUSION
Columbia Commons/Columbia Hicks brings together people from all walks of life into a single community, housing renters who earn less than 80 percent of AMI and homeowners who project much higher on the income scale. The diversity of income in such a desirable neighborhood would have been difficult without the innovative condominium structure—which is becoming standard practice in developments with complex financing—and the strong partnership with the city.

Lessons from Industry Leaders

Tel Metzger, Project Manager
Columbia Commons/Columbia Hicks Apartments
New York, New York

RICHARD ROSAN: What makes this project different from other projects L&M has developed?

TEL METZGER: What is remarkable about this building is that it represents so much innovative development and partnerships to get it to work. When we first took our idea to the different city agencies, they said, "This has never been done before. You can't do this. It will never work."

ROSAN: Could you please outline the unique elements, starting with the land?

METZGER: There were two flag lots. One was city owned, the other privately owned. We purchased the privately owned lot and worked with the city to purchase the public land, which had a requirement to build affordable housing.

Cobble Hill is largely a landmarked area. So the availability of new-construction apartments for entry-level purchasers was almost zero.

ROSAN: The subdivision of the land seems very complicated, but vital to the project.

METZGER: We have six condominiums, which we call master condominiums. The rental building has two condominiums; one is a tax-credit condominium and the other was for affordable rentals. That one was segregated from the tax-credit condominium because the tax-credit investor did not want to be exposed to the risk. There was one condominium for the two for-sale buildings. In the basement, there are three parking condominiums, each associated with a separate residential building.

ROSAN: How unusual is this condominium scheme?

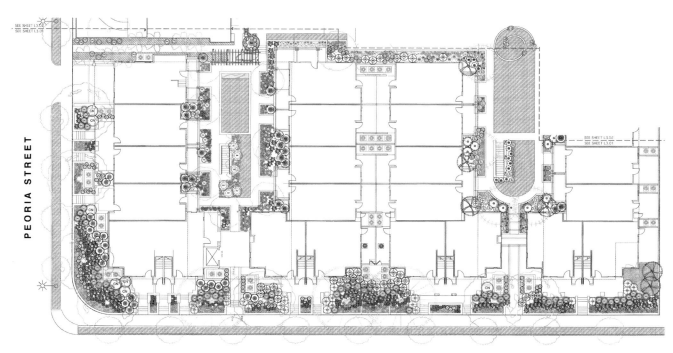

PEORIA STREET

FAIR OAKS BLVD.

structures, freeing up space for a new courtyard and eliminating surface parking at the project. Although expensive—the developer estimates that this decision added $2 million to the development cost—the move allowed HPP to build more units and add much-needed open space.

All the units at Fair Oaks Court were constructed at market rate with market-rate amenities. HHP focused on energy and water efficiency by including energy-efficient windows, insulation, appliances, and low-flow toilets, all elements that allow the development to exceed California energy code requirements by 56 percent. HHP partnered with the city of Pasadena's Department of Water and Power to share the additional cost of energy-efficient upgrades to Fair Oaks Court.

To create contextual new construction, HHP's architects took their design cues from the neighborhood surrounding Fair Oaks Court. The area features a wide range of early 20th-century home styles, including Arts and Crafts, Spanish Revival, and Victorian. The four new, three-story structures were built in an Arts and Crafts style. HHP rehabilitated the historic homes on Fair Oaks Court by cleaning and refinishing the original claw-foot bathtubs, preserving and repairing built-in cabinetry where possible, choosing period-appropriate fixtures and paint colors, and restoring enclosed porches to promote a community feel in the development. All the historic homes are now protected by conservation easements and are eligible for local landmark status, further protecting the historical integrity of Fair Oaks Court and its neighborhood.

CONCLUSION

HHP finds true success in the diversity of Fair Oaks Court residents: five families are multigenerational, the oldest homebuyer is 82, and the youngest is 24. All these buyers had access to solidly constructed and well-designed homes within their price range. Fair Oaks Court allows these homeowners to have a stake in the community in which they live and work. The new and old construction at Fair Oaks Court blends seamlessly in an appropriately scaled homeownership development that combines historic context and affordability.

Lessons from Industry Leaders

Catherine Boland
Charles Loveman
Heritage Housing Partners
Pasadena, California

RICHARD ROSAN: New Markets Tax Credits were integral to this project. Explain to me how they work.

CHARLES LOVEMAN: First, your project has to be in the right census tract, median income–wise. The NMTC is a tax credit of 39 cents for every dollar that is invested in a project. We went to the city of Pasadena and proposed that if it put in the money—not as a direct loan to us, but as a loan to a tax-credit entity that will make the loan to us—we would get 39 cents in tax credits for every dollar the city puts in. So with the city putting in the $4.1 million loan, we received an additional $1.5 million in tax credits. We were then able to sell those credits to an investor at 70 cents on the dollar.

ROSAN: How much public subsidy was necessary to make this project feasible?

LOVEMAN: $4 million of subsidy in the form of the low-interest loan was from the city, $3 million from the NMTCs, $1 million from the state, and $1.5 million from the county of Los Angeles.

ROSAN: So we're close to $10 million?

LOVEMAN: For a $20 million project, basically cutting the cost in half.

ROSAN: So that covered the land cost. How did your nonprofit acquire the land?

LOVEMAN: We were able to persuade our seller to be very patient. We went through the approval process with the city and got approved for the $4 million loan. The city put its money in first. So we bought the land with city funds.

We also had an acquisition loan for about half the land from the Enterprise Foundation. Then the city put in a second acquisition for the second half. The city then paid out its money. Once we received the construction loan, we paid back Enterprise.

ROSAN: How did you finance the total construction, the $20 million?

LOVEMAN: The county and state money ($2.5 million) did not come in until completion, so we had to finance our way to that point. Washington Mutual provided a traditional loan of $8.2 million out of the $20 million we needed. Between the deferred developer fee and title escrow fees that get paid out, we needed to finance about $18 million. And the $2 million or so was part of the costs that were deferred until closing.

ROSAN: How as a not-for-profit developer do you get some outside funding to support your work?

LOVEMAN: We apply for grants. The Enterprise Foundation and Bank of America have given us money. The Washington Mutual Foundation was also very generous to us. But some years you get money, and some years you don't. The grants were for $50,000 to $75,000. I'm in my eighth year now. When I came, the organization spent an enormous amount of time applying for grants. I went to the board and said, "We're going to either make it or not make it, but we're going to do it as a developer."

ROSAN: So do you make a develop-ment fee?

LOVEMAN: Yes. We make about $25,000–$30,000 per unit. Our pro forma for this project was a $1 million developer fee ($25,000 per unit). We probably came in at $900,000 or so. We came pretty close to that number, given how much longer it took to sell the units than we thought. We got our certificate of occupancy in May 2008, and we got our permission from the state (selling subdivided land is highly regulated in California) in July.

We sold our first unit in July 2008, while the real estate crisis hit the fan in October/November. Washington Mutual, which we had designated as the preferred lender for the homebuyers, called us up one day and said, "We're gone." We had everybody in escrow for all our units, and the lender just disappeared. So it took a long time to close.

ROSAN: Explain a little about the underground parking garage, which to me is one of the most unique aspects. How did you manage to have almost no surface parking on a nearly two-acre lot and put it all underground?

LOVEMAN: We were originally going to put surface parking near the renovated buildings. But in a presentation to one of the city council committees here in Pasadena, a council person who had been a schoolteacher and was very sensitive to many of the young families and kids said, "There's no play space." We quickly got into a discussion about the fact that to create play space, we would need to put the parking underground—a costly decision.

ROSAN: What was the extra cost?

LOVEMAN: About $2 million altogether, with the garage and open space. So when you figure it all out, maybe it was a $1–$1.5 million incremental increase to push the parking underground. But then the flip side was we could add more units aboveground. So it's really a $2 million cost, and you pick up one-half to three-quarters of a million dollars in extra revenue. And so you're at $1 to $1.25 million.

ROSAN: What is your unit cost?

LOVEMAN: We built this project for $195 per square foot hard cost (including the garage), and the average unit size is around 1,100 to 1,200 square feet. One-bedrooms are between 750 and 850 square feet.

ROSAN: What is the income of the residents?

CATHERINE BOLAND: When we sold these units, the area median income was $54,200 for a family of four.

LOVEMAN: For the workforce units, it's 80 percent of that number—approximately $40,000. Low-income is about 50–80 percent of the median. Those buyers are making between $25,000 and $40,000. Our two-bedroom units sold for about $125,000.

ROSAN: Is that still a stretch financially for these families?

LOVEMAN: We made a deal—mostly thanks to Cathy's efforts—with the state. Before last year, the California Housing

ROSAN: Are property taxes a big issue?

BOLAND: Property taxes are an issue. But we worked closely with the county tax assessor, and we were able to get that office to understand the way the sales price is calculated. The assessor should not include all of those soft, silent mortgages that basically subsidize the unit. It's highly restricted. In terms of an assessor, he or she wants to tax whatever is the fair value. The taxes match the downpayment and the first mortgage. That's how the county sets it. But it would be astronomically high if it were to tax it at the full value.

LOVEMAN: We had two concepts. We had an affordable sales price and the contract price. You take that $10 million of subsidy that we talked about, $3 million of which is tax credit, so that doesn't go on the title, but the $7 million that represents the city, county, and state money all goes on the title. So $7 million divided by 40 units is about $200,000 per unit. If the affordable price is $225,000 for a moderate-income two-bedroom unit, we add another $200,000 of silent debt, so that the price is $425,000. The price the buyer is paying with financing is $225,000, so it's a big deal to get the assessor to say, "We're only going to tax you on the $225,000, not on the $425,000."

ROSAN: What do you do about resale?

LOVEMAN: The title has restrictions that basically say you cannot sell it at market rate.

ROSAN: Is that a deed restriction?

LOVEMAN: Yes. It's a 45-year deed restriction.

Finance Agency had tax-exempt mortgage pools. We bought $10 million worth of mortgages at 5 percent, 30-year fixed money, so those households are getting a very low interest rate.

ROSAN: Did the city require you to develop for homeownership?

LOVEMAN: When Fuller Seminary approached us and we thought we could make a bulk deal with Fuller to sell all or most of those units, the city reminded us that we had promised that it would be homeownership.

So we sold the units to Fuller Seminary for full price. Then the seminary turned around and sold the $850,000, six-bedroom unit for $300,000 to faculty members. And they put a $550,000 second loan on it.

ROSAN: What about sustainable features?

LOVEMAN: Pasadena has its own utility, Pasadena Water and Power Department, and we made a deal with it up front. We'd figure out what the cost was to design to code, and then we'd figure out what the cost was to design to an energy upgrade. And whatever the cost difference was, we'd split it 50/50. That was about $200,000—we put in $100,000 and the utility put in $100,000. We used two-by-six framing instead of two-by-four framing, so that we could put in more six-inch insulation. We have R19 insulation along exterior walls, R30 insulation in the ceiling, and all low-UV windows. We have all energy-efficient appliances and the HVAC equipment is highly energy efficient.

ROSAN: If owners want to sell their units, what do they do?

LOVEMAN: Two things happen. When you want to sell your unit, we have a first right of refusal to buy it at the future affordable price. You bought it at $225,000, and two years from now it is $240,000; we'll buy it at $240,000, so you'll make $15,000 plus whatever you paid down and so forth from the principal. That's the first option: we'll buy it at the affordable price, and we'll assume all that secondary debt, so you don't have to buy that off. You just need to pay off the first. If we don't exercise that right of first refusal, then you can sell it at market price, but there are equity share provisions that basically say up to 50 percent of the profit is going to go back to the city, county, and state.

ROSAN: Is there some time limit?

LOVEMAN: The way we structure it, the profit is split between public agencies and the owner. It's a tricky balance because we don't want people to profit unfairly from all this public money. But one of the things that is different between affordable homeownership and affordable rental is that we do want people to have an equity stake.

ROSAN: So they know that every year they stay here, in a certain sense their equity is increasing.

LOVEMAN: In fact, 15 years is sort of our rule. We'll exercise our right of first refusal up to 15 years. And after 15 years, our sense is that you've earned equity and paid your mortgage every month so you should benefit. And that way you are not always a low- or moderate-income household. You get money out of owning a house.

GEORGE MARTELL

"You often hear folks who don't want the increased development complaining, 'It stresses our schools, our infrastructure.' The idea here is to help offset those impacts."

—Lisa Alberghini

The Hayes at Railroad Square

Haverhill, Massachusetts

In the heart of the Merrimack Valley, the Hayes at Railroad Square is an innovative historic rehabilitation of two contiguous mills listed on the National Register of Historic Places.

ALAN MYERS

PROJECT DATA

Developer
Planning Office for Urban Affairs Inc.
Boston, Massachusetts
www.poua.org

Public Partner
City of Haverhill
Haverhill, Massachusetts

Design Architect
The Architectural Team
Chelsea, Massachusetts
www.architecturalteam.com

Housing Information
Total number of units: 57
Workforce rental units: 19
Affordable rental units: 33
Market-rate rental units: 5

Occupancy Rate of Workforce Units: 95%

Project Affordability
50% AMI   1 BR = $800; 2 BR = $950
60% AMI   1 BR = $940; 2 BR = $1,100
80% AMI   1 BR = $1,125;
                  2 BR = $1,325–$1,350
Market   1 BR = $1,250;
                  2 BR = $1,425–$1,500

Area Median Income, 2011–2012
60% $54,960
100% $91,600
120% $109,920

Development Cost
$20.1 million

Development Timeline
Date acquired: June 2008
Date started: October 2009
Date rentals opened: August 2010
Date completed: September 2010

Case Study

Located just one block from the Haverhill commuter rail station, the Hayes, a 57-unit apartment building, was one of the first workforce housing projects to take advantage of Massachusetts's Chapter 40R program, which encourages transit-oriented development. Working in concert with the city of Haverhill, which is dedicated to the revitalization of its downtown area, the Planning Office for Urban Affairs (POUA) provides 19 one- and two-bedroom apartments for households making between 60 to 120 percent of the area median income (AMI), 33 units for residents making less than 60 percent of AMI, and five units for market-rate renters.

THE PROBLEM

The Boston region has a richness of jobs, human and institutional capital, and high-tech and research capacity, but its housing stock, neighborhoods, and towns have some of the highest housing costs in the nation. Much of the Boston area is built out, and many of its desirable communities close to jobs and transit offer very limited opportunity for the construction of more modern densities that would create affordability. In the town of Haverhill, the local Department of Community Development estimates that 20 to 30 percent of its households making between 60 and 120 percent of AMI have moderate or severe housing cost burdens.

THE SOLUTION

POUA, a nonprofit housing developer affiliated with the Roman Catholic Archdiocese of Boston, was able to take advantage of one the country's most sophisticated smart growth development programs: Chapter 40R. The statute provides significant incentives for localities to create smart growth districts around transit that promote higher densities and allow expedited permitting for developers. In return, localities receive incentive grants tied to the number of units that are built in a 40R district, provided that at least 20 percent of all units built remain affordable for 30 years.

Haverhill's Downtown Smart Growth District is one of the commonwealth's most successful Chapter 40R districts, with more than 500 units created under the code in the five years since its adoption. The Hayes at Railroad Square was the first project permitted under the program and stands out among these developments because it successfully targeted both workforce and affordable housing markets, rather than just satisfying the 20 percent affordable set-aside requirement.

POUA used a variety of incentives and financing packages to achieve affordability, including (1) density bonuses for transit-oriented development, (2) historic tax-credit equity proceeds, (3) brownfield grants, (4) a partial charitable donation that lowered the land acquisition cost, (5) below-market debt financing, and (6) an innovative land swap with the transportation authority to construct a parking garage for residents.

PEABODY PROPERTIES

THE PRODUCT

The 80,000-square-foot project is the historic rehabilitation of two mill buildings, one constructed in 1894 and the other in 1911, which once housed a box factory for the shoe industry and was a major employer in Haverhill. The building's historic integrity was retained during renovations, which involved facade masonry repairs, restoration of the storefront wood framing, and the original smokestack.

The one- and two-bedroom affordable and workforce units were leased at two price points: affordable units for those making less than 60 percent of AMI and "moderate/market" for those making between 60 and 120 percent of AMI. Nineteen of those moderate/market units were restricted to workforce housing, with five units left unrestricted.

The apartments are designed to have a loft-style feel, boasting such original features as large windows, exposed-beam ceilings, and decking. The ground floor features three commercial spaces—two of which are occupied by local business owners—and a community room, laundry room, fitness center, and children's play area. Parking is provided in an adjacent structured lot, which was enabled by a land transfer with the local transportation authority. The project sits on a one-acre parcel, which is within walking distance of the train station, in a walkable historic downtown that is home to restaurants, small businesses, and an arts district.

CONCLUSION

The development met with strong market absorption, leasing at a rate of 14 units per month, even in a district that has added more than 500 affordable and market-rate units in the last five years. The success of the Hayes at Railroad Square shows the power of Massachusetts's Chapter 40R program when embraced by a locality determined to revitalize its downtown and increase affordability and a developer with the technical capacity to develop and finance housing for moderate-income families. The development has added daily economic activity and pedestrian traffic to an area of Haverhill that has not seen business activity in decades and was the leader in the redevelopment of downtown Haverhill, which has now seen more than 500 units built or under construction.

Lessons from Industry Leaders

Lisa Alberghini, President
Bill Grogan, Chief Operating Officer
Planning Office for Urban Affairs Inc.
Boston, Massachusetts

RICHARD ROSAN: This project really had the strong support of the town of Haverhill. Can you tell me about the partnership?

LISA ALBERGHINI: The mayor of Haverhill has an extraordinary goal to revitalize the downtown area and business district. Haverhill was a mill town, a mill city built particularly around the shoe-manufacturing business, so it had a lot of old buildings. The Hayes building manufactured boxes for packaging shoes. In 2006, the mayor got all his different city departments in one room and invited brokers, developers, and other real estate folks to come into that room for a developers' conference. You could literally walk around the room and talk to the planning director and get information from him, talk to the Public Works Department, or go to a broker's table and say, "Show me what you've got," and they would show you five listings. So the city was very active in bringing in developers to revitalize the downtown area.

ROSAN: What other tools did the city have at its disposal?

ALBERGHINI: The city had established what in Massachusetts is called a Chapter 40R zoning district, an overlay district designed to encourage transit-oriented development. If you are a city in Massachusetts and you establish a 40R district, the developments within that district are allowed greater density and parking ratios. Around 2006, Haverhill was concentrating its district around the train station.

BILL GROGAN: At the end of 2006, the city formalized the 40R zoning district,

GEORGE MARTELL

which was approved by the state. The establishment of the zoning district enabled the permitting path, the very simple permitting path for this building as well as other buildings within the 40R district.

ROSAN: What incentive does the city have to create these districts?

GROGAN: There is a monetary incentive for a city to do this: upon adopting a 40R district, a city is entitled to a onetime payment. Then, for each additional unit that is built within the district over and above what is allowed in the underlying zoning, the city receives a per-unit payment. In Haverhill's case, it was $600,000 in total.

ALBERGHINI: You often hear folks who don't want the increased development complaining, "It stresses our schools, our infrastructure." The idea here is to help offset those impacts.

ROSAN: So this is a historic mill building in a historic downtown—what was involved in the rehabilitation process?

GROGAN: The rehab required a complete gutting of the inside, as well as brownfield remediation on two parcels adjacent to the building that were part of the property. The building needed a full asbestos abatement, lead abatement, and conversion from a former mill building.

ROSAN: What is the residential mix of the buildings?

GROGAN: There are 11 one-bedroom units, 40 two-bedroom units, and then a balance of five two-bedroom duplex units.

ALBERGHINI: There are also three retail spaces on the ground floor. It was very important to the city that there be a retail presence on the ground floors of all the streets in downtown; in fact, it's a requirement in a 40R district. Two of the retail spaces are currently leased, one to an optometrist and one to an interior decorator.

ROSAN: Are there any sustainable elements?

GROGAN: In addition to the reuse of a historic building, our green efforts centered on high-efficiency boilers, low-flow toilets, highly insulated windows, and high-efficiency laundry and other facilities.

ROSAN: Tax credits were an essential part of this project. What was that challenge like?

GROGAN: The first level of tax credit is federal Low-Income Housing Tax Credits to support 33 units that are being rented below 60 percent of the area median income. Those came from an allocation of tax credits from the State Department of Housing and Community Development ultimately sold to our low-income housing tax-credit investor bank, Bank of America.

For the federal historic tax credits, we needed to get the buildings placed on the National Register [of Historic Places] since we were just outside a historic district. In support of that application was the age of the buildings, built in 1894 and 1911. But they were also of significance because of their historic value as part of the shoe industry here in Haverhill. In total, tax credits made up approximately $12 million of the $20 million development cost.

ROSAN: You received a long list of grants and incentives—when it was all said and done, you only had to go to the bank to borrow how much?

GROGAN: For the construction financing, it was $11.5 million from Bank of America, and for the permanent financing, it was approximately $2 million from the Massachusetts Housing Partnership Fund. All the money we needed came from loans, soft loans, or grants. Construction was approximately $125 a square foot.

ROSAN: The historic tax credits require that it has to be a rental for five years. Is that correct?

ALBERGHINI: Right. After the five years, the workforce units can be turned into condominiums. We would retain control of the 33 low-income tax-credit units. But they aren't separated: the 19 workforce units that could be converted into condominiums are interspersed throughout the development, which is important from a mission perspective to really create a diverse integrated community. For example, we have some of the market-rate units on the seventh floor as well as some of the affordable units up there.

ROSAN: Was the parking garage financed differently?

GROGAN: That was financed through a couple of different sources. It was being built by the Merrimack Valley Regional Transportation Authority through a federal earmark grant with state matching of funds, with private developers purchasing spaces in the garage on a long-term lease basis. With over 500 units coming into the downtown area, the owners of those buildings are purchasing spaces. So those purchases and the public and private money are financing the garage construction.

ALBERGHINI: The parking garage is another interesting example of cooperation between the city and POUA. We had site control over the Hayes building and a parcel across the street that the city needed for the parking garage. So we worked to swap that parcel with the city so it could get the parking garage closer to the commuter rail station.

ROSAN: So you worked with the city in a number of venues.

ALBERGHINI: The city has a lot to do with this. The mayor is very, very proactive. He brought us here to the developers' conference. We worked with the city on the parking garage, the 40R process, and a fast-track permitting process. We've looked at four other buildings in the last month and put offers in on two of them.

"[He] grew up in Brookline but had to move out about five or six years ago because they couldn't afford to live here. Now, he's been able to move back to town."

—Lisa Alberghini

The St. Aidan

Brookline, Massachusetts

The St. Aidan's 36 new affordable units were created as part of a mixed-income infill project in the town of Brookline, Massachusetts, a suburb of Boston.

PROJECT DATA

Developer
Planning Office for Urban Affairs Inc.
Boston, Massachusetts
www.poua.org

Public Partner
Town of Brookline

Design Architect
Antonio DiMambro + Associates Inc.
Boston, Massachusetts
www.dimambro.com

Landscape Architect
Bellalta 3 Design
Brookline, Massachusetts
www.bellalta.com

Housing Information
Luxury condominiums: 9
Market-rate condominiums: 14
Workforce condominiums: 16
Affordable rental units: 20

Occupancy Rate of Workforce Units: 100%

Project Affordability
Purchase price: $157,500–$177,000
Rent: $800–$1,800

Units Reserved	Household Income
6	Less than 30% AMI
7	Less than 50% AMI
7	Less than 60% AMI

Area Median Income, 2011–2012
60% $54,960
100% $91,600
120% $109,920

Development Cost
$37,728,000

Development Timeline
Date acquired: September 2002
Date started: May 2008
Date opened: January 2009
Date completed: March 2010

The St. Aidan project is an adaptive use of an abandoned, but historic, two-acre church property. Opening in 2010, the St. Aidan was the largest affordable housing effort in the town in many years, and it has helped Brookline near the 10 percent affordable housing goal mandated by the Commonwealth of Massachusetts. The church building itself was restored as nine luxury condominiums and was complemented by three new buildings, housing 50 additional units. Those 50 units include 16 workforce condominiums affordable to families earning 80 percent of the area median income (AMI), and 20 rental units that are capped to be affordable for families earning 60 percent of the AMI. The affordable units were made possible by the internal subsidy from the 23 market-rate units.

The St. Aidan was developed by the Planning Office for Urban Affairs (POUA), a nonprofit affordable housing developer affiliated with the Archdiocese of Boston, whose mission is to serve as a catalyst for social justice through its work in housing development, neighborhood revitalization, and affordable housing advocacy. Public and private subsidies, a significant land sale discount, increases in density, fee waivers, below-market debt financing, special regulatory approvals, and permanent affordability restrictions have allowed Brookline to house more people that work and serve within the community.

The St. Aidan is near two Massachusetts Bay Transportation Authority light-rail lines, Brookline's award-winning schools, several hospitals, universities, and other major employers. Shopping and services are within walking distance. This proximity to important destinations helps make it a sustainable and walkable development.

THE PROBLEM

A community of 57,000 residents, Brookline is a desirable place to live and work because of its proximity to Boston, its accessibility to public transit, and its location near Boston University, Northeastern University, and numerous top-notch hospitals. However desirable, Brookline is one of the nation's most expensive housing markets, and people who work in the town are frequently priced out of the community. The median single-family home price in 2009 was $1,169,250, and the median price of condominiums was $451,000. These prices are generally out of reach for teachers, police officers, fire personnel, and other service workers. Exacerbating Brookline's housing affordability problem has been the lack of new housing: the number of new units in Brookline from 1980 to 2000 was less than one-third the number created between 1960 and 1980.

PRESERVATION

The National Register of Historic Places' designation of the church posed a challenge to the development of St. Aidan. Built in 1911, the Tudor-style church was the baptismal place of President John F. Kennedy and was the Kennedy family's parish for years. Many neighbors, including several who had worked on the National Register nomination in the 1970s, were hesitant to allow the church to be altered to accommodate new condominiums. Their resistance persisted even though the church had been abandoned since 1999 and was at risk of full demolition by another developer. Those neighbors engaged the developer in a six-year legal battle despite the late senator Edward M. Kennedy's stating that there was no better way to honor the legacy of the parish and his brother John than creating a diverse community that would bring opportunity to those living there. Through a series of compromises, the

suit was settled in 2006, and the plans that were executed in 2009 and 2010 were finalized.

The developers were cognizant of the importance of preserving the open space and existing trees as well as the church building itself. The St. Aidan was built around a landmark 150-year-old copper beech tree with a half-acre canopy, as well as several other older trees. The developers also preserved significant open space on the property; some was kept private for its residents, and some, including an original pedestrian thruway, remained open to the public.

THE SOLUTION
POUA was able to take advantage of many fortuitous financial incentives to move forward with the development of the St. Aidan. The unprecedented $6.2 million commitment from the town of Brookline consisted primarily of a loan from the Brookline Affordable Housing Trust, which is funded by local developments without affordable components. Other local funds included HOME and Community Development Block Grant (CDBG) allocations. POUA also received Low-Income Housing Tax Credits from the Massachusetts Department of Housing and Community Development, and funds from MassHousing, Federal Home Loan Bank of Boston, Bank of America, and Wainwright Bank. Its plans relied on Chapter 40B, the state's affordable housing zoning law, which allows developers to negotiate significant flexibility in zoning provisions if less than 10 percent of the town's housing stock qualifies as affordable. Through this statute, the developer was allowed to build 59 units, almost six times more than what would have otherwise been permissible.

The St. Aidan's affordability was made possible in part by the below-market price of the land, provided by the Catholic parish. This discount was a clear indication of the parish's support for the mission of the development, especially as it had other offers for the property of nearly double the amount of POUA's.

The affordability of the St. Aidan is supported through a residential property tax exemption for the first $150,000 in real estate value, and a deed restriction on the workforce townhouses secures them as affordable below 80 percent of AMI.

THE PRODUCT
The four buildings of the St. Aidan complement the adjacent uses on each side of the site and vary in scale, materials, and massing. They are sited carefully to allow public allées and plazas to blend the new development into the well-established urban neighborhood. The development is designed to foster community, with common bike storage, pathways, and a central courtyard to be used by residents for informal gatherings, picnics, and children's play space. The 66-unit parking facility has been provided underground to minimize its effect on the site. The underground parking and the reserved scale of the new buildings succeeded in preserving open space, sight lines, pedestrian access, and several trees.

CONCLUSION
The St. Aidan was a victory in finding balance between important, but sometimes opposing, community priorities. As a community, Brookline looked to promote affordable development while preserving neighborhood quality of life, open space, and the public realm. It shared

the goal of preserving a historic artifact in the St. Aidan while maintaining social and economic diversity in the town. POUA's development was able to find the middle ground and respects the character of the surrounding residential community, while allowing for higher density and affordable options. It serves as a model for adaptive use that creates opportunities for working families in a job- and transit-rich setting.

Site Map

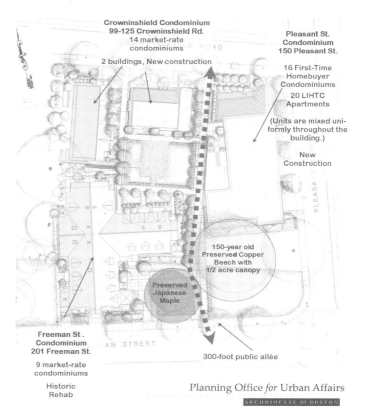

Crowninshield Condominium
99-125 Crowninshield Rd.
14 market-rate condominiums

2 buildings, New construction

Pleasant St. Condominium
150 Pleasant St.

16 First-Time Homebuyer Condominiums

20 LIHTC Apartments

(Units are mixed uniformly throughout the building.)

New Construction

150-year old Preserved Copper Beech with 1/2 acre canopy

Preserved Japanese Maple

Freeman St. Condominium
201 Freeman St.

9 market-rate condominiums

Historic Rehab

300-foot public allée

Planning Office *for* Urban Affairs
ARCHDIOCESE OF BOSTON

Lessons from Industry Leaders

Lisa Alberghini, President
Planning Office for Urban Affairs Inc.
Boston, Massachusetts

RICHARD ROSAN: First, can you describe your organization.

LISA ALBERGHINI: We are a social justice ministry affiliated with the Archdiocese of Boston and a nonprofit developer. Our office was formed about 40 years ago. We have developed 2,500 units of affordable and mixed-income housing. We specialize in a number of things, one of which is building affordable housing in affluent communities to provide an opportunity for people to have access to the amenities and benefits in those types of communities and to live there when they wouldn't otherwise be able to afford to.

ROSAN: Talk about this project in particular—the history, the church, the Kennedys.

ALBERGHINI: This is roughly a 1.8-acre site. It had a church, a rectory, a couple of old garages, and a lot of asphalt. But the church was special in that it's on the National Register of Historic Places; it was the Kennedy family church when the kids were growing up. Both JFK and Robert Kennedy were baptized there. Ted Kennedy was still living when we were developing this project. And he said that there was no better way to honor the legacy of the parish community, his brothers, and the work they spent their lives doing than to help others in need and to develop affordable housing.

Because of the complexity of retaining and retrofitting the church, we really had to build luxury condos because it was so costly. And we could only fit nine units—so there are nine units in the church. And then there are 14 new-construction townhouse units and 36 units in our mixed-income building, which is a brick three- to five-story building. Also, the site included a landmark copper beech tree that took up more than a quarter acre on the southeast corner. So between the church and the copper beech tree, they take up about 35 percent of the site. Consequently, there was relatively little left to develop on the site.

ROSAN: This is an outstanding location.

ALBERGHINI: We're a quarter mile from two major subway lines on Beacon Avenue and Commonwealth Avenue. We are about one-third mile from Longwood Medical Center, which is where some of the most internationally renowned medical facilities are: Harbor Cancer Institute, Beth Israel, Brigham Women's, Children's. . . . We are a quarter mile from Boston University and the Charles River, and a little farther than that from Harvard, but nearby. We are within a mile of Fenway Park. And we are in a true residential neighborhood. Also, we are on this amazing corner of a commercial district, which has a wonderful collection of stores. It's one of *the* places to be if you live around here. The other thing that attracted us is the school system. Brookline in general has internationally renowned schools, but Devotion School, which is the school in this district that we belong to, is—even in Brookline—one of the best. And for us to be able to bring in lower-income residents and first-time homebuyers and give them access to this school system is really amazing.

ROSAN: Let's review the mix. We have nine luxury condos in this church building. It's quite amazing all the work on the exterior of this landmark church. And the condos are really luxury.

ALBERGHINI: They're priced from $1.2 to $2 million. There are 14 wood-frame units in two buildings that are market-rate condominiums: seven one-bedrooms and seven three-bedrooms.

ROSAN: And you have 36 affordable units.

ALBERGHINI: It's 36 condominiums, 20 of which were sold to a tax-credit investor and 16 of which were sold to individuals who were first-time homebuyers, 80 percent of AMI.

ROSAN: What are the incomes in the community?

ALBERGHINI: Up to $70,000. We have a development that's 70 percent local preference for both the workforce and the tax-credit units. And so the people renting them truly live in town, work in town. . . . The child over there, Maurice, his dad grew up in Brookline but had to move out about five or six years ago because they couldn't afford to live here. Now, he's been able to move back to town. His kids are going to the school he went to when he grew up. So a lot of people are coming back. We have a fair number of children, which makes the courtyard lively.

ROSAN: And are the market-rate homes all sold?

ALBERGHINI: We have two remaining. The one-bedrooms sold the fastest. I think we couldn't have built enough one-bedrooms in retrospect.

ROSAN: The site is beautiful because there isn't a car on it anywhere. So how many parking spaces do you have?

ALBERGHINI: Below grade are 66. We also have two handicapped spaces.

ROSAN: And they had to be squeezed into this piece of land on which you can't touch the church or the tree.

ALBERGHINI: We tell people, "Wherever there isn't a church or a tree, there is a garage."

ROSAN: So you had a huge cost. Do you have a sense of what a garage costs?

ALBERGHINI: Our estimation is close to $55,000 per space. It's difficult because part of the garage formed the foundation of the mid-rise building. It was a complicated garage: a tight site, a lot of shoring up needed to be done on the streets.

ROSAN: How did you subsidize the workforce and affordable units?

ALBERGHINI: We had a combination of resources. First, we paid an estimated 70 percent of market for the land. But it was only permitted for ten homes, and that would have meant tearing down the church. And then we got three grants from the town: We have townhouse funds—low consortium funds coming through the town. We have funds from the town that come from a commercial linkage program; when you build an office building, you have to donate so much to this housing fund. We also have $0.5 million of CDBG money that was used to help keep the tree. And so, together those town funds are a little over $6 million.

ROSAN: The project pays taxes, however, to the town.

ALBERGHINI: The 23 market-rate units probably pay on average around $8,000. So that's about $200,000–$300,000 per year. The apartments pay around $1,200 in taxes. And the workforce units—

there is a town program to encourage affordable first-time homebuyers, so it excludes the first $50,000 of value. So they are taxed on $28,000.

ROSAN: What about sustainability? Did you do anything special?

ALBERGHINI: We score well on the commonwealth's sustainable development principles, in part because we are reusing an existing resource. So the fact that we kept this church and retrofitted it really is a way to develop sustainably. And it's a very walkable neighborhood, so many residents don't have cars.

ROSAN: How did you convince the town to get to this density?

ALBERGHINI: It was a negotiation. We actually had hoped for more. First, there's a law special to Massachusetts—Chapter 40B—that allows affordable housing developers to override local zoning and build at higher densities. We

could have been granted more density still. It was a negotiation. We like to do what we call "friendly 40Bs," where we work with communities rather than being overly aggressive. So we had a long, multiyear conversation. We said to the town, "We're happy to work with you, but we have an objective and mission that we want to meet. And to the extent we can meet that, we will lower the density." We would not give up on the affordable units, and that's why it's 60 percent affordable. And there is quite a range of lower-income to $2 million condos. But when they wanted to lower the density, we told them what it would cost. If we eliminated 14 or more market units, or ten market units, it's going to cost X. And so through this process, when they wanted us to keep the church, keep the tree, have a brick facade, put the parking underground, and have fewer units, we said we would do that, but we would cut back on the market units.

ROSAN: How did you finance the project?

ALBERGHINI: It was complicated. There were four condominium associations: the master condominium and three lower-tier condominiums. The master condominium owns the garage and the common areas. Then there's the church condominium, which is the luxury condominium; the condominium of the new wood-frame construction; and the condominium that is the mid-rise building. In the mid rise there are 36 units, 16 of which are individually owned and 20 of which are owned by a partnership that benefits from the tax credit. So you have multilayers of financing. We had multiple financial partners.

ROSAN: And the total cost?

ALBERGHINI: $38 million. But that was skewed by the luxury condos for sure.

We talked about the money from the town. We also had money from the commonwealth—I want to say we had four sources of money.

ROSAN: Is it replicable?

ALBERGHINI: We've replicated ourselves—Rollins Square [an earlier project] was very similar. We could name a half dozen developments very similar in structure. It's what it takes to do infill development in an affluent market. Infill is inherently complex, and the kind of structure flows from that. And it's inherently expensive, and the financial model flows from that.

ROSAN: I understand there was a legal challenge from neighbors.

ALBERGHINI: Well, one neighbor led the charge and got other people to sign on. The interesting thing was that the town was supportive—100 percent. It was also interesting because there was less interest in the church as a historic landmark until we were going to build affordable housing here and considered taking it down. Then, there was a lot of interest in the historic nature of the church, and people wanted to keep it and not have it become affordable housing. We got our approvals. And the abutter can take you to court. And the abutter can add several plaintiffs. They sued the town, the zoning board, and the developer. At that point, it's a detail, but we had to go back to the ZBA [Zoning Board of Appeals] a second time. Under the law, the ZBA determines whether the modification is minor or major. If it's a minor modification, it doesn't have to reopen the public hearing. The Board of Appeals made that decision. The abutters appealed on the grounds that the change was not a minor modification, but was major. So that took three years.

ROSAN: Is there any neighborhood reaction now?

ALBERGHINI: They love it. We started this development back in 2002. We started construction for real the second time in 2008. So we had been on it ten years before it was done, and you get to know everybody pretty well. And they said it's beautiful. One day, one of the neighbors who had been challenging walked by. And I said to this older woman, "What did you expect? This is what we told you it would look like." They just didn't believe it.

ROSAN: I think it's also history. Thirty years ago, affordable housing was not a very attractive neighbor.

ALBERGHINI: But now they know the people. A gentleman in one of the first-time homebuyer units has been in the habit of shoveling a woman's sidewalk. She lives in one of the high-end market-rate homes there and she's elderly, and people take care of her.

Design Solutions

Workforce housing entails a holistic approach, where design and construction play an integral role. Aesthetic and functional considerations generate processes that support mitigating environmental impacts, cost-saving opportunities, or neighborhood integration and urban identity.

PROJECTS

500 Hyacinth Place
The Cottages at Longborough
The Kalahari
South City Lights

"We wanted it to be a beacon—for people to see the turbine and say, 'That's Highland Park.' That's what Highland Park is about—it's about green technology; it's about innovative technology. And that's basically what happened."

—David Brint

500 Hyacinth Place

Highland Park, Illinois

The first of its kind in Chicago's affluent North Shore, 500 Hyacinth Place is a small-scale, infill affordable workforce housing development that serves as a model for communities where land cost is prohibitive and affordable housing scarce.

PROJECT DATA

Developers
Brinshore Development LLC
Northbrook, Illinois
www.brinshore.com

Housing Opportunity Development
Corporation
Techny, Illinois
www.hodc.org

Public Partner
City of Highland Park

Design Architect
K2 Architects
Chicago, Illinois
http://k2arch.com

Landscape Architect
Guy Scopelliti Landscape Inc.
Libertyville, Illinois
www.guyscopelliti.com

Housing Information
Workforce homeownership townhouses: 10
Affordable rental units: 4

Occupancy Rate of Workforce Units: 100%

Project Affordability
Purchase price: $165,000–$239,000

Units Reserved	Household Income
1 rental	50% AMI
3 rental	60% AMI
3 homeownership	80% AMI
7 homeownership	120% AMI

Area Median Income, 2011–2012

60%	$45,240
80%	$60,300
120%	$90,480

Development Cost
$4,680,000 (no land costs—donated by the city)

Development Timeline

Date acquired:	May 2007
Date started:	October 2007
Date opened:	January 2009
Date completed:	March 2009

In October 2007, for-profit developer Brinshore Development and nonprofit developer Housing Opportunity Development Corporation (HODC) broke ground on 500 Hyancinth Place—an environmentally sustainable, 14-unit affordable workforce housing development in the city of Highland Park, Illinois. The development is in proximity to a commuter rail line, a bus route, primary and secondary roadways, bicycle paths, a park, and a variety of restaurants and stores. The site is approximately one mile from Lake Michigan to the east, Route 41 to the west, and the Highwood restaurant corridor to the south.

Located within Chicago's affluent North Shore corridor, the development—which includes ten for-sale townhouses and four rental apartments, all of which are occupied—aimed to address the shortage of affordable workforce housing in the area. Highland Park has had a historical commitment to housing inclusiveness and serves as a model municipality for creating affordable housing opportunities for working families. All units within the development are targeted to households earning between 50 and 120 percent of the area median income (AMI).

THE PROBLEM

In 1997, the city of Highland Park embarked on a planning process to update its comprehensive master plan. During the process, increasing concern arose about the lack of affordable housing opportunities and its negative effect on the city's tradition of inclusiveness. That concern was precipitated by rising land and housing costs, as well as by the redevelopment and gentrification that were occurring in the central downtown district. That trend resulted in the loss of much of the city's more modest, affordable housing stock—especially rental units.

In November 1998, the city council directed the City of Highland Park Housing Commission to prepare an affordable housing plan to be incorporated into the city's master plan. With assistance from the University of Illinois at Chicago's Voorhees Center for Neighborhood and Community Improvement and Great Cities Institute, the housing commission studied nationwide examples of affordable housing best practices and selected those most relevant to Highland Park. In January 2001, the city council adopted the resulting Affordable Housing Needs and Implementation Plan. The plan recommended several strategies designed to complement each other, including inclusionary zoning and employer-assisted housing. Additional strategies included the establishment of the Highland Park Illinois Community Land Trust (now known as the Community Partners for Affordable Housing) and the Demolition Tax and Housing Trust Fund.

THE SOLUTION

Brinshore Development and HODC successfully acquired multiple layers of public, private, and nonprofit funding from a variety of sources to secure the development budget and to reduce the sales and rental costs of the units. Many of these agencies have special setasides for nonprofit organizations, so the involvement of a nonprofit owner or developer was necessary to secure those funds. The funds lowered effective sales prices, thereby reducing the burden on families purchasing the new homes.

One of the central development objectives of Hyacinth Place was to create long-term affordable workforce housing. All stakeholders worked in close cooperation to design and execute the development plan. A variety of strategies were used to reduce initial project costs, and additional techniques were used to maintain long-term affordability. The city of Highland Park was an instrumental partner throughout the development process and provided vision, leadership, and material contributions. The land was acquired by the city of Highland Park and was contributed to the development through a donation to the land trust. The land trust serves as the permanent ground lessor to guarantee that the homes and apartments remain affordable. This guarantee is accomplished by the land trust's retaining ownership of the land and selling to qualified buyers at affordable prices while leasing the land through a ground lease at a nominal fee. Resale restrictions require that the homes be offered to the land trust or an income-qualified buyer at a formula price that keeps the homes affordable in perpetuity. Additionally, homeowners share the appreciation of their homes over time—equity participation (or shared equity) allows owners to share in the appreciation of their units and will provide long-term affordability for future generations of homeowners. The land trust also owns and manages the four affordable rental units in the development.

In addition to reducing initial development costs, the donation of land to a nonprofit opened an opportunity to create a "soft" source of funding through the Illinois Donation Tax Credit. Moreover, the city's implementation of an Inclusionary Zoning Ordinance permitted the development of three additional units above and beyond what was allowed by right. Because the Inclusionary Zoning Ordinance was already in place, it decreased the time, complication, and difficulty in seeking additional density. The city also assisted by waiving permit fees, saving the project an additional $237,718. Most funding sources for this project are typical for affordable housing development and therefore make this type of project replicable.

The developer pursued additional methods to establish affordability, including an employer-assisted housing designation, which allows the assignment of priority to Highland Park residents and employees, including teachers, nurses, civil servants, police officers, firefighters, grocery employees, and retail employees. Occupants of Hyacinth Place include three teachers, two retail employees, two telecommunication employees, one civil servant, one park district employee, one legal assistant, one nonprofit employee, one nurse, and two retirees. As evidenced by the residents' occupations, the development has been very successful in achieving its workforce target.

THE PRODUCT
Formerly the location of a commercial office building, the infill site is approximately three-quarters of an acre. Zoning allows 15 units per acre (11 on three-quarters of an acre), but three additional units were permitted because of the affordable density bonus permitted by the city's Inclusionary Zoning Ordinance. The development includes 14 architecturally sensitive, sustainably designed dwelling units: ten 1,600-square-foot homeownership townhouses with attached garages and four 1,200-square-foot flats with surface parking. Units include two or three bedrooms and two or two and a half bathrooms. Seven of the homeownership units are targeted to families earning 120 percent of AMI. The three remaining homeownership

units are reserved for families earning 80 percent of AMI. The rental units are targeted to households whose incomes do not exceed 60 percent of AMI.

Achieving a LEED for Homes Gold certification, Hyacinth Place's environmentally sustainable design incorporates geothermal heating and cooling, a wind turbine for electricity generation, permeable paving to control stormwater runoff, an energy-efficient building envelope, Energy Star appliances, renewable flooring and finish materials, nontoxic paints and stains, reflective roofing materials, and landscaping that incorporates native plants to minimize water usage. In addition, patio pavers are coated with photocatalytic "smog-eating" cement (TX Active cement), which includes a titanium-dioxide catalyst that attracts and neutralizes noxious emission gases caused by the burning of fossil fuels. These pavers actively scrub the air of the gases responsible for smog and acid rain. These design features have reduced the project's energy consumption, thus lowering overall housing costs for owners and renters on an ongoing basis.

The buildings were sited to face the street and sidewalk, with all garages located on the rear courtyard, hidden from street view. The garage placement eliminates the need for multiple curb cuts, which protects the pedestrian environment, increases safety for children and those walking past the buildings toward the Fort Sheridan train station, does not disrupt the public parking, and creates an environment conducive to children's play and neighbor interaction. This site layout uses the existing public alley to increase efficiency and maximize green space.

The architecture was designed to be sensitive to the existing character of the neighborhood in scale, massing, and materials. An extensive neighborhood architectural survey was conducted to ensure compatibility with existing buildings and housing stock. Additionally, the design incorporated

contemporary elements to reflect the inclusion of forward-thinking sustainable technologies.

Strong vertical elements unify the individual townhouse facades and counterbalance the significant width of the Hyacinth elevation. The bay elements provide a texture and rhythm to the streetscape, as well as creating sheltered, private entryways and providing dramatic interior space. The use of brick and concrete on the exterior takes its cue from the neighborhood, reinforces the level of high-durability construction, and, most important, will withstand the extremes of the northern Illinois climate, thus reducing long-term maintenance costs.

CONCLUSION
Affordable housing allows working families to remain within the community, maintains economic and cultural diversity, and provides homes for essential employees. 500 Hyacinth Place is representative of how a small-scale, infill affordable workforce housing development can be designed and implemented in an affluent community where land costs are high and affordable housing scarce. The land's $2 million appraised value demonstrates the challenge of creating affordable housing without the support of the municipality. The city of Highland Park helped pioneer innovative affordable housing planning and development on Chicago's affluent North Shore by creating the mechanisms, structures, and community support that allow a development of this character to proceed. This project is a model private/public collaboration of a municipality, a for-profit developer, a nonprofit developer, and a community land trust.

Lessons from Industry Leaders

David Brint, Chief Executive Officer
Brinshore Development LLC
Northbrook, Illinois

RICHARD ROSAN: Tell me about Highland Park.

DAVID BRINT: Highland Park is an upscale community—an extremely upscale community. Lake Forest is just to the north. And the rest of the North Shore is to the south of this area. But this development's being done in Highland Park is unique because most high-end communities don't support workforce housing, they don't support affordable housing, but Highland Park is a little bit different. They've had issues in the past with trying to make housing available to people who work in the community, and people who want to stay in the community.

Another important element is inclusionary zoning. For example, when people get divorced, the family splits up. The parents can't both afford to live in Highland Park, and the children get displaced. So inclusionary zoning addresses that problem.

ROSAN: Tell me about your inclusionary zoning. How did that work?

BRINT: Basically, for every development that's over six units, there is a requirement to have one affordable unit, and the project gets a development bonus.

ROSAN: Tell me more about the project.

BRINT: Hyacinth Place is a transit-oriented development that sits right across the street from the metro line, which takes you all the way to the city. It will take you all the way up to Waukegan, so you could work in major companies north of here, or you could work in the city. We also incorporated something this neighborhood has never seen—sidewalks.

People from all over this neighborhood would walk to the metro in the street. When we went to put in sidewalks, at first they fought us; now, they love it because they walk down the sidewalks.

ROSAN: Tell me about the signs on the property.

BRINT: We let the community know what the green technologies were. So four signs on the property highlight each of the major green technologies in the development. First of all, each unit is heated with geothermal HVAC.

ROSAN: You had to build wells.

BRINT: Each unit has a well—about 700 feet down. It is a long way, but you have to get surface area around the tubing. I think they brought close to a 45 percent reduction in utility costs for a typical 2,200-square-foot townhouse.

ROSAN: Impressive.

BRINT: Even with the windows, our values are high. So we gave a lot of attention to materials to help control utility costs. This development has 14 units. There are ten for-sale units and four rental units. On the rental units, you want to try to control utility costs. Three of the ten for-sale units were sold to people under 80 percent of the area median income; seven were at 120 percent of the area median income.

ROSAN: What are the residential taxes?

BRINT: The residential taxes here are probably 1 and 0.75 percent of assessed value.

ROSAN: So $8,000 for $500,000.

BRINT: Yes.

ROSAN: What families have moved in?

BRINT: We found exactly what we had hoped—somebody from public works, a teacher from one of the middle schools that had a young child, two divorced-parent families, and a couple of folks that work in the community.

ROSAN: Explain some of the green features.

BRINT: We used permeable pavers. And we used something that had just come to the states—photovoltaic pavers. And they actually absorb nitrogen.

ROSAN: What do they do?

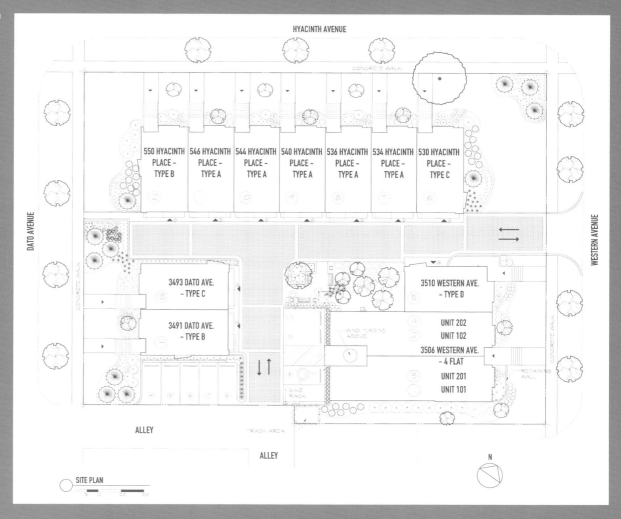

BRINT: Cars basically kick out carbon dioxide gases into the area here. And normally they just sit on the pavement, which gets dirty. These pavers actually stay white because they absorb the nitrogen, compound it with another component, and send it out as some form of oxide.

ROSAN: Never heard of that—interesting.

BRINT: Now the other good thing that you haven't noticed yet is the wind turbine unit.

ROSAN: Where is it?

BRINT: Exactly. It runs enough electricity for all the exterior lighting. And that was the goal: to provide the electricity so the association doesn't have to.

ROSAN: I've never seen that kind of design. I wouldn't even know that it was a wind turbine.

BRINT: Right. And one of the reasons that we wanted it was because this property is very visible when you're driving up. We wanted it to be a beacon—for people to see the turbine and say, "That's Highland Park." That's what Highland Park is about—it's about green technology; it's about innovative technology. And that's basically what happened.

ROSAN: What kind of heating system do you have in here?

BRINT: Geothermal.

ROSAN: So there's no air conditioning?

BRINT: No, geothermal works both heating and cooling. Actually, the air conditioning is easier because the

ground is 55 degrees. So when the water comes up, it's cooled to 55 degrees.

ROSAN: I did not see any compressors.

BRINT: That's the advantage of geothermal—no compressors. It is a tube that has a glycine-water mixture, so it doesn't freeze. The tube goes down into the ground and goes back up. When it gets down into the ground past 42 inches, the mixture turns to 55 degrees and comes back up as 55-degree water. Then it goes over filament and you can cool it pretty easily.

The technology is the other way around in the wintertime; a heat exchanger removes the cool and takes the heat.

ROSAN: Cost wasn't prohibitive? There are 14 of them, aren't there?

BRINT: It's probably $10,000 more per unit, whereas a normal blower system would probably cost $6,000 per unit. This system is probably $15,000 or $16,000 per unit.

ROSAN: It won't have to be replaced?

BRINT: It will never have to be replaced. The only things to be replaced are heat pumps, the pumps that circulate, so their maintenance costs are extremely low. The utility costs are extremely low. So if you can afford the front-end funding, it's great.

ROSAN: Tell me about how you bought the land.

BRINT: It was the Highland Park Housing Commission. The housing commission actually owns other affordable housing properties. They generated the money. They bought the property from the city, which made everybody happy. That's

their job, to create more housing. They bought the ground and then we told them what we were going to do. They went up for an RFP [request for proposal] and we came back with a green project, which is something new.

ROSAN: You still own the rentals?

BRINT: Our nonprofit partner will keep the rentals. They run it—four units are easier for them to run than it is for us. And so they were funded by varying branches of financing. It included some home funds, some trust funds from the state, a small first mortgage, some grants from the Illinois Department of Economic Development, Center for Neighborhood Technology. We layered all of these units.

ROSAN: So what's the real cost and how much was subsidized?

BRINT: The cost was probably $250,000 a unit. And the real economics under it are probably $35,000 a unit. So the subsidy is $200,000 and change in order to make these deals work. We rent these units probably for an average of $900 a month, which is $11,000 per year. It costs $4,000 in expenses, maybe $4,500. That takes you down to $6,000. And you always want a debt coverage ratio, so you've got $5,000 to service debt. So you're borrowing $50,000 a unit, and there's $200,000 of subsidy in order to make the rentals work.

ROSAN: How about the sales?

BRINT: We sold them for $239,000. It probably cost $325,000–$340,000. And the fact that there's no land cost with that—the city contributed the land—really compensated for it. So it was a lot easier to make that work. There was probably a 20 percent subsidy.

ROSAN: So what would you think the premium for the green was?

BRINT: Ten percent. Unfortunately, a lot of times that 10 percent is the profit in the deal. That's why they're willing to do it.

ROSAN: It's a shame you couldn't have built more units.

BRINT: Well, we tried to take a look at doing that. If the market turns around completely and we get these price points back up in the area of $500,000, then we might try to pursue it, because everybody seems to love it. It was kind of nice. Even the neighbors who opposed it vehemently—when it was done— most of them came back and said, "We were wrong."

"You have to be a risk taker. The government
had to be entrepreneurial here."

—**Richard Rosan**

The Cottages at Longborough

Charleston, South Carolina

The Cottages at Longborough were built as part of a 14-acre urban revitalization project located 2.5 miles from downtown Charleston, South Carolina.

PROJECT DATA

Developer
The Beach Company
Charleston, South Carolina
www.thebeachcompany.com

Public Partners
City of Charleston
Lowcountry Housing Trust

Design Architect
Neil Stevenson Architects
Charleston, South Carolina
www.neilstevensonarchitects.com

Housing Information
Market-rate condominiums: 82
Workforce condominiums: 42

Occupancy Rate of Workforce Units: 100%

Project Affordability
Purchase price: $102,625–$150,875

Area Median Income, 2011–2012
60% $37,320
100% $62,200
120% $74,640

Development Cost
$5,576,622

Development Timeline
Date acquired: December 1999
Date started: December 2000
Date opened: June 2009
Date completed: Summer 2009

The Cottages at Longborough were developed as a public/private partnership with the city of Charleston. The overall development comprises 82 market-rate luxury single-family homes and 42 affordable workforce condominium homes. The city of Charleston agreed to allow the Beach Company to demolish Shoreview, a blighted 1950s-era public housing development, and replace it with a mixed-income community.

Following the design and construction by the Beach Company, the entire workforce housing side of the project was purchased by the city of Charleston for a predetermined price of $125 per square foot. The city worked with individual purchasers, applied combinations of available financial tools to arrange mortgages, and resold the workforce units at cost to qualified homebuyers.

The Longborough subdivision, of which the Cottages are part, is located in the Wagener Terrace neighborhood of northern Charleston, South Carolina. Hampton Park, the Citadel, and a Charleston Area Transportation Authority bus stop are community assets within walking distance of Longborough. Charleston's downtown area and historic district, the Medical University of South Carolina, the College of Charleston, and the South Carolina State Ports Authority are all within 2.5 miles of the project site. The site is well situated among transit arteries, within one mile of both Interstate 26 and U.S. Route 17. Longborough is ten miles from the Charleston International Airport, which increases its accessibility.

THE PROBLEM

This centrally located site had been home to a dilapidated and failing public housing complex. In addition, Charleston has an insufficient affordable housing supply, and many potential homebuyers are priced out of the market. In 2009, the median home price was $192,000, significantly higher than many working-class residents can afford. During the design and construction phases of the Cottages, the city assembled a waiting list of several hundred people who expressed interest in living there, underscoring the need for supplying more workforce housing in Charleston.

THE SOLUTION

The Cottages at Longborough were made possible by a public/private partnership, waived utility fees, creative amendments to the Longborough Planned Development District (PDD) standards, purchase price subsidies, special financing rates, creative deed restrictions, and the donation of capital and services by the private and public sectors.

The City of Charleston Department of Housing and Community Development selected qualified purchasers and coordinated mandatory homeowner education classes for the Cottages. After the private developer had executed the design and plans for the development, the city of Charleston purchased all of the workforce units and subsequently resold the individual homes to qualified homebuyers for $102,625 to $150,875. The workforce homes have a density of 26 units per acre and occupy a 1.6-acre marsh-front parcel in the Longborough subdivision. The project's public/private partnership worked to amend the existing PDD standards to maximize density through the elimination of minimum lot size and setback criteria.

By designating on-site parking areas as "public alleys," future maintenance costs fall on the city of Charleston as opposed to the Cottages owners. Because the site had previous utility connections to serve the Shoreview public housing complex, Charleston Water Systems waived tap and impact fees on water and sewer connections.

Each purchaser at the Cottages receives funds from the city of Charleston to be used toward closing costs, mortgage reduction, and POA (property owners association) reserves. The homebuyers are provided loans from the Lowcountry Housing Trust, a private sector nonprofit community development financial institution, or CDFI, that supports affordable housing, and three private sector lenders: Atlantic Bank, First Federal, and BB&T. Qualified buyers also receive a First-Time Home Buyer Tax Credit of $8,500 from the U.S. government.

Deed restrictions on the workforce units ensure the future affordability of the Cottages. The restrictions tie resale prices to future median family income and the consumer price index in the Charleston Standard Metropolitan Statistical Area and require future buyers to meet city qualification standards.

THE PRODUCT

Designed by the public/private partnership of Neil Stevenson Architects and the Charleston Civic Design Center, the Cottages at Longborough are two- and three-bedroom units built in a quad format that preserves the overall scale and character of the surrounding neighborhood of single-family homes. Units at the Cottages feature individual entries, private porches, HardiePlank cement fiber siding, and architectural

details that blend with the southern style of the Longborough subdivision.

The Longborough subdivision is pedestrian-friendly in the new urbanist model, with homes facing the street, separated from the sidewalk by only a small frontyard. Grand oak trees along the sidewalks were carefully retained during the construction process. Raised front porches enliven the street while affording some separation and privacy. The development includes public parks with trails and a crabbing dock.

The Cottages feature energy-efficient products, such as low-E insulated windows, high-efficiency 13 SEER HVAC units using 410a Freon, programmable thermostats, Energy Star–rated

appliances, insulated ductwork, insulated fiberglass entry doors, and full batt insulation in walls and ceilings.

The project consists of three building types that were designed with standardized bathroom and kitchen configurations and were constructed multiple times to increase construction efficiency. The developer used its national account to purchase complete appliance packages at discounted prices, saving the project money. Innovative construction techniques include Hurri-Bolt structural bracing, engineered floor trusses to facilitate HVAC ductwork, and two-hour fire-rated commercial shaft wall separation between units.

CONCLUSION

The Cottages at Longborough provide new housing options for Charleston's working class. Along with the rest of the Longborough subdivision, the Cottages are an architecturally cohesive, high-density, pedestrian-friendly urban neighborhood that speaks to the city's historical context.

Lessons from Community Leaders

Joseph P. Riley Jr., Mayor
Charleston, South Carolina

RICHARD ROSAN: Tell me about the project.

MAYOR RILEY: The land where Longborough sits was once a privately owned affordable housing development. It was financed in the 1950s, but there was no ongoing subsidy. It was low-income housing that had served its time. It was no longer cost-effective for the Beach Company and it needed substantial work. And the land had become quite valuable. So from the private sector standpoint, the right thing to do was to demolish the development and redevelop the land for housing.

ROSAN: Was there any restriction on that land?

RILEY: No. The family built the development and operated it for all that time, and so it had been in continuous ownership.

ROSAN: How did you relocate the people who lived there?

RILEY: We worked with the Beach Company, which was very cooperative. It was a business decision they had to make. But there was community outcry because people had lived at Shoreview a long time, and for many of them, it had been good housing. So we worked with ShelterNet, a nonprofit affordable housing entity, to help relocate the people and find Section 8 and affordable housing for them.

From the very beginning, we felt it was important that a portion of that land be redeveloped for affordable housing, from a historical and from a justice standpoint. And we considered acquiring the land—which would have been through condemnation—to make it public. But the first problem was the numbers wouldn't work because the

a state-of-the-art 18,046-square-foot squash center in the South Building managed by StreetSquash, a local education enrichment provider. Accessory parking for 62 cars is located below grade.

In a nod to the neighborhood's ethnic heritage, the patterned facade is inspired by South African Ndebele tribal designs. *Adinkra* symbols, West African icons representing concepts like wisdom, unity, and perseverance, adorn the columns, and a sculpture by El Anatsui, a Ghanaian artist, hangs in the lobby.

GREEN DESIGN
The transfer of development rights, low land cost, and cross subsidy from the sale of market-rate units allowed the project to be built to high-quality standards with energy-efficient features, which in turn allow for healthier living and increased savings for the residents. The condominium project harnesses wind, solar, and hydrogen-generated energy and combines sustainability and design excellence. Features include high-performance lighting fixtures, green roofs, Energy Star appliances, bamboo-strip flooring, and luxury furnishings created with sustainable materials. In addition, a fresh-air filtration system continually purifies interior air throughout the building. During construction, the builders used recycled materials in everything from the structural steel and concrete to the gypsum board and carpets. In total, the sustainable design elements are expected to reduce homeowners' energy expenses by 21 percent, and savings passed on to the tenants is estimated at $1,200–$1,300 per year compared with a standard building.

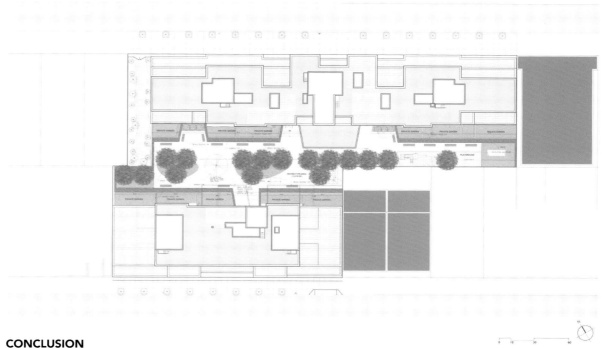

CONCLUSION
The Kalahari stands as an important model not only for creating home-ownership opportunities for working families in a high-cost area but also for promoting healthy living for a demographic that suffers disproportionately from poor air quality and recreation options. A booming housing market and a low land acquisition cost contributed to the project's success, but an innovative joint venture that was able to transfer development rights and increase density made the high ratio of workforce units—half of the 249 total residences—viable. The small upfront investment in sustainability features translated into marketability for the project and long-term cost savings for the resident owners.

Lessons from Industry Leaders

Carlton Brown, Chief Operating Officer
Full Spectrum of NY
New York, New York

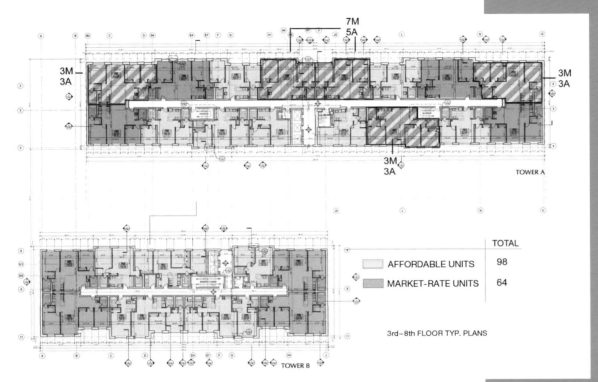

7M
5A

3M
3A

3M
3A

3M
3A

TOWER A

	TOTAL
AFFORDABLE UNITS	98
MARKET-RATE UNITS	64

3rd–8th FLOOR TYP. PLANS

TOWER B

RICHARD ROSAN: How did you decide to develop a joint RFP with L+M Development Partners?

CARLTON BROWN: I knew Ron Moelis, head of L+M, through the New York City Housing Partnership. We are both involved in building affordable housing in New York City. When the RFP came out for the Kalahari site, we met with Ron and talked about some reasons why we might work together. L+M is a larger company than we are, and it was better known to HPD. It just made sense to do a partnership.

ROSAN: What made you adopt such an innovative approach at the Kalahari?

BROWN: We were looking to do something that more directly addressed people's needs in Harlem. For instance, for us, putting in music practice rooms was really important. We found from past developments that many of the kids played instruments and the noise passed right through the wall. The walls aren't soundproof and people complain; so I thought, why don't we put in music rehearsal rooms? That adds value. Why don't we do wireless Internet? That adds value because we're selling to young people. Why don't we bring in fiber optics and give broadband and include it in the cost?

ROSAN: Did that drive up the cost of the apartments?

BROWN: No, but it involved more planning and design on the front end. For instance, you do things to reduce your energy consumption by making a better wall. You don't really spend more money; you just design it differently. You do things like installing the insulation and vapor barrier in the right place, and suddenly you've increased the performance of the wall by 60 percent. We built a tighter building envelope and used superior glazing, low-E, and better R-value, across the windows and across the walls. There are no electrical outlets on the outside wall and no air leaks—little things like that don't cost anything.

ROSAN: What are some of the other sustainability features in the Kalahari?

BROWN: We take a whole-systems approach to our buildings. We try to create an efficient building that has as little waste as possible. We used water-source heat pumps, and because the building envelope is tighter, the air-conditioning and heating systems can be smaller. And I can get a smaller system that's higher performing at the same cost of a larger system that's lower performing. Since the walls and envelope are sealed, we need to deliver and filter fresh air. We also use a heat recovery system with the bathroom and kitchen exhaust, so when the exhaust passes through, it preheats the fresh air that comes into the apartment. So you're recovering energy. Ultimately, the goal is to create affordability throughout the building's life cycle. If you do it well, you can actually reduce your costs by building a better-performing building.

ROSAN: Do you have a green roof?

BROWN: We have three green roofs: one large one that works as a courtyard and two smaller ones at the ninth-floor setback. It gives our residents a nice outdoor space, and it costs only an additional $7–$8 a square foot on top of your roof. So you pay a little more for that, but we saved money in other places. We used high-percentage recycled content and materials and they didn't cost us anymore. Where it did cost us some time was in the record keeping and getting subcontractors to keep track of it.

ROSAN: What advice can you give to developers of workforce housing?

BROWN: The approach for every project is going to be different from the Kalahari. Although there are some best practices to be learned from everything we did: from the way the financing was structured to the way we reached out to the community and the way we tried to focus on sustainability, not just from the environmental standpoint, but from the economic standpoint. It was critical to sit down with the community board and say we want an agreement that says we'll give preference to 50 percent of Harlem residents first. When we made our presentation to the community board, we said, "We're going to do the community preference," which turned out to be a green building.

ROSAN: Why do you think the Kalahari was so successful?

BROWN: A lot of projects in Harlem have not done well. The Kalahari units sold even when the market was tanking. We really wanted to make a distinct product, something that would have value in good times and bad. Other developers built mostly 700-square-foot one-bedroom units that they thought they could sell for $1,000 a square foot in Harlem, which just wasn't going to happen. We built a project for families; our apartments have two and three bedrooms with a few that have one bedroom.

ROSAN: What would you do differently on your sustainability issues if you did it again? Did you learn some lessons?

BROWN: One of the things we did was to have a lot of enhanced data and communications services and building control systems. They're all separate systems. So when you come to the data closets, there's this gaggle of wire that goes all over. If you think about it from a sustainability standpoint, it's a whole lot of wasted wire because a lot of it could have been carried on a single fiber-optic cable. We could have had more integrated services that probably would have cost less if we had planned more on the front end. We would try to have a better approach to interrelated communication and data services.

Another thing I would do differently is I would not build with the same superstructure system and wall system. We have plank on bearing wall construction there, and I probably would have used structural steel and prefabricated panels. I think we would have built the building more quickly.

ROSAN: Have you sold out all the units?

BROWN: Yes. Everything sold, even in a down market. We sold them for $700 a square foot. The thing that I really like about it is if you go down there on a Saturday or after work, when people are back home, you see that it's really a community of people. And that community looks like the global community our city has become. You go through and you can see that the music practice rooms have been reserved. People are really using them. Come through in the afternoon and you see kids in the two meeting rooms doing homework and other kids helping them with it. I think L+M and Full Spectrum are both really proud of the Kalahari because it really changes the standard for what housing can be in this community and because so frequently people build buildings, but they don't enhance the fabric of the community.

Lessons from Industry Leaders

Ron Moelis, CEO
L+M Development Partners
New York, New York

RICHARD ROSAN: Let's talk about the genesis of this project.

RON MOELIS: We had done a number of affordable homeownership developments in Harlem, and this was an opportunity to take that to the next level. We had developed other market-rate projects, but most of what we had developed was fee based because there wasn't really a market. With the Kalahari, we realized that there was a market for this housing, but the price of the land affected our ability to build these projects.

ROSAN: Did you receive any density bonuses or entitlements?

MOELIS: The city did a rezoning itself before it disposed of the land. We bought air rights from Full Spectrum, our partner, which came from a property it owned next door. Buying these air rights increased the size of the project significantly, which was one of the things that helped our RFP application because we had about 80 feet of air rights that we were able to add on. We paid about $4 million for that, and we were able to do more affordability and more market rate in the Kalahari.

ROSAN: What were some of the challenges?

MOELIS: Timing is everything, but that's true in any real estate deal. We had a good relationship with our partners, but it was challenging in the beginning for all of us. We came from different corporate cultures and had different goals. I think their goals were very different from ours in some ways, so we really took a lot of time getting up to speed. Our partners were very heavily involved in green construction. We came to a very good middle ground. We got LEED certification that was Silver as opposed to Platinum; we cut out some of the bells and whistles. That was a challenge, but we worked through it. The mixed-use component was also challenging.

ROSAN: What advice would you give to other workforce housing developers?

MOELIS: One should be very careful. We were lucky with the timing of the sale of the workforce units. It was easier for workforce buyers to get financing before, and now it is much more restrictive. I think if I were doing things again, I would be very careful.

"America's homebuilders are back to doing entry-level housing at price points that working families can afford."

—Con Howe

South City Lights

South San Francisco, California

South City Lights features 280 stacked flat condominiums built over a partially sunk podium garage.

PROJECT DATA

Developers
Watt Communities
Santa Monica, California
www.wattcommunities.com

CityView (Joint Equity Partner)
Los Angeles, California
www.cityview.com

Public Partner
City of South San Francisco

Design Architect
KTGY Group Inc.
Irvine, California
www.ktgy.com

Housing Information
Market-rate for-sale units: 213
Workforce for-sale units: 67

Occupancy Rate of Workforce Units: 100%

Project Affordability
Purchase price: high $200,000s–high $600,000s

Area Median Income, 2011–2012
60% $57,240
100% $95,400
120% $114,480

Development Cost
$115 million

Development Timeline
Date acquired: April 2005
Date started: Phased
Date opened: December 2006
Date completed: November 2008

Developers had been passing over South City Lights' 13-acre infill site in South San Francisco for many years. Because of its unusual shape and steep topography—the grade changes up to 70 feet in places—it had been left as underused space in this densely developed and growing city. Working together, Watt Communities and CityView took on the challenging site and were able to find a cost-effective way to develop it through the provision of necessary retaining walls and the phased construction of six four-story buildings with unobstructed views of San Francisco Bay. South City Lights features 280 stacked flat condominiums ranging from 828 to 1,337 square feet.

The development is located in South San Francisco, a major employment center anchored by United Airlines, Genentech, See's Candies, and over 80 biotech firms. Only 15 minutes from San Francisco, the area is ideally located and well maintained: schools and neighborhood and regional shopping are within minutes of the project.

Working with the city of South San Francisco, the developer secured entitlements for a density of 20 units per acre in exchange for restricting the sale of 67 units to families earning between 80 and 120 percent of the area median income (AMI). This exchange of density for affordability allows private developers like Watt and CityView to build workforce housing without direct public subsidies.

THE PROBLEM

The city of South San Francisco, with its working-class history of steel mills and manufacturing, has developed into the highest concentration of biotech firms in California. Its need for workforce housing is exacerbated by its location in one of the most expensive housing markets in the nation. By 2004, the median home price in San Mateo County was $660,000, with San Francisco's prices even higher. The city is in great need of housing that is affordable for its working-class residents.

The developer faced a significant engineering challenge: the site's steep and unstable slope. An added challenge was the work needed to reinforce the soil had to be done while avoiding the regional power lines at the top of the site. Disturbing those lines in any way could have led to high repair costs and damages.

THE SOLUTION

South City Lights' affordability was achieved by careful site selection development, cost containment, and cooperation by the local jurisdiction on entitlement, density, and implementation of the below-market-rate units. To be permitted at a feasible unit density, the developers went through a lengthy entitlement process. They were allowed to build at 20 units per acre higher than the surrounding area but were restricted to a design that ensured continued views from the adjacent properties. The new condominiums represent a new product type in an area of single-family homes and townhouses. In exchange for the high density, South San Francisco required 25 percent of the units to be priced to sell to families at 80–120

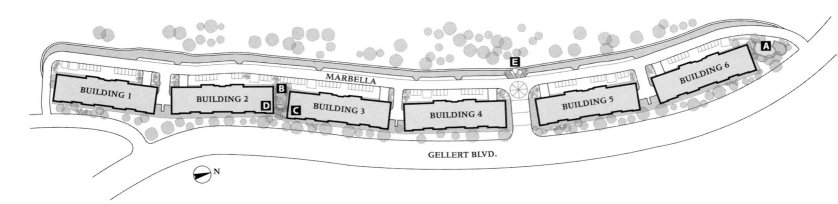

A FITNESS CENTER   **B** CLUB HOUSE   **C** TOT LOT   **D** BARBEQUE AREA   **E** WATERFALL

percent of AMI. Resales of the below-market-rate units are governed by the city's rules, including the right of first refusal, in order to ensure continued affordability.

A partnership of the builders, the city of South San Francisco, and a regional joint power authority is providing buyer assistance for those purchasing affordable units. Bay Area HomeBuyer Agency through its administrative arm, First Home Inc., provided low- to moderate-income, first-time South City Lights buyers with a number of valuable resources and services. Those services include downpayment assistance from the city of South San Francisco, the California Housing Finance Agency, and the Federal Home Loan Bank WISH Program; mortgage credit certificates; up to 103 percent financing; extensive homebuyer education workshops; and one-on-one homebuyer counseling to assist in the home-purchasing process. These assistance programs allowed some below-market-rate buyers to obtain over $125,000 in assistance and some households with incomes as low as 60 percent of AMI to securely purchase a home.

THE PRODUCT
Located at the intersection of two major boulevards, Gellert and Westborough, South City Lights is an infill location in the heart of a jobs-rich community. The site is 15 minutes by interstate highways from downtown San Francisco and five minutes from San Francisco International Airport. The newly extended BART system is quickly accessible, with a commuter shuttle bus going from South City Lights to the station. Nearby are a variety of restaurants, a seniors' living center, a grocery store, and other neighborhood services and businesses.

The units at South City Lights were designed to be appealing with finishes and amenities that allowed a "natural affordability," such that even the market-rate units were sold at $100,000 less than the median home price for the region. All six buildings have been completed and are selling for prices ranging from $265,000 to $414,000 for income-restricted units and $379,000 to more than $600,000 for unrestricted units.

To overcome the difficulties with the steep site, the developers engineered an innovative, but well-tested, "soil nail wall." Drilling into bedrock to hang concrete on the side of the slope proved to be a more economical solution than the traditional method of digging deep footings and layering one portion of the wall on the next. The wall has attractively textured, terraced retaining elements and a large waterfall feature.

CONCLUSION
South City Lights is a successful work-force housing development because of its infill location on a difficult site, the city's cooperation with entitlements and implementation, and its affordability by design. The project proves that provided these replicable conditions, the private sector can still produce new, for-sale, workforce housing without public subsidies, even in one of the nation's most expensive housing regions.

Lessons from Industry Leaders

Con Howe, Managing Director
Los Angeles Fund at CityView
Los Angeles, California

RICHARD ROSAN: What is the most important lesson from this project?

CON HOWE: For me, the most important thing about the project is the fact that it was all done without direct public subsidy. It really comes back to the private sector: America's homebuilders are back to doing entry-level housing at price points that working families can afford. And that's ultimately why I think this project is a good example, because it didn't have any direct public subsidy.

ROSAN: Were there any requirements from the city?

HOWE: In fact, the city required that 20 percent of the units were affordable for low- and moderate-income families. That requirement was part of the entitlements. Northern California has a lot of communities that have inclusionary housing requirements. And each municipality has some difference in when the requirements kick in. The South City Lights project needed a rezoning and it needed entitlements from the city. As part of that, the city required 20 percent to be low and moderate income (in this case, it went from 80 to 120 percent of AMI).

ROSAN: Why was this site "overlooked"?

HOWE: The site had been left over from a highway construction project. It was too steep to build on, but it is 13 acres outside San Francisco. There are all sorts of these leftover sites in the postwar suburbs. You're not going to find the nice, rectangular ten-acre site in these neighborhoods, so the challenge here is to figure out how to build on them in a cost-effective way.

ROSAN: How did you manage to develop market-rate units that are still cheaper than the median home price in the region?

HOWE: Because the project is much denser: it's 20 units to an acre. I know there had been proposals years ago for a row of townhouses just lining the highway. But no one, as I understand it, before our team could figure out a way to engineer it. It was also a question of how to bring down the cost for the land and bring up the density to something you can build efficiently. Whoever had been designing townhouses before couldn't make it work, but we came up with an effective engineering solution.

ROSAN: So your argument here is that this is a run-of-the-mill project that is unusual in that it is a leftover site?

HOWE: Some people might shy away from that, but we don't. We finance a lot of stuff that has no requirement. But we only finance entry-level housing, so we don't do luxury housing, and we actually don't do tax-credit or affordable housing. So we're in that niche.

The other thing about this community is that it has some of the highest housing costs, and a lot of jobs—and a lot of these people are commuting (like Genentech's employees and all those other companies in the area), so it really was workforce in that sense. And the other thing is—and I think this goes back to getting ULI builders that are experienced and know how to do this— they had to figure out the engineering, they had to be as cost-effective as possible.

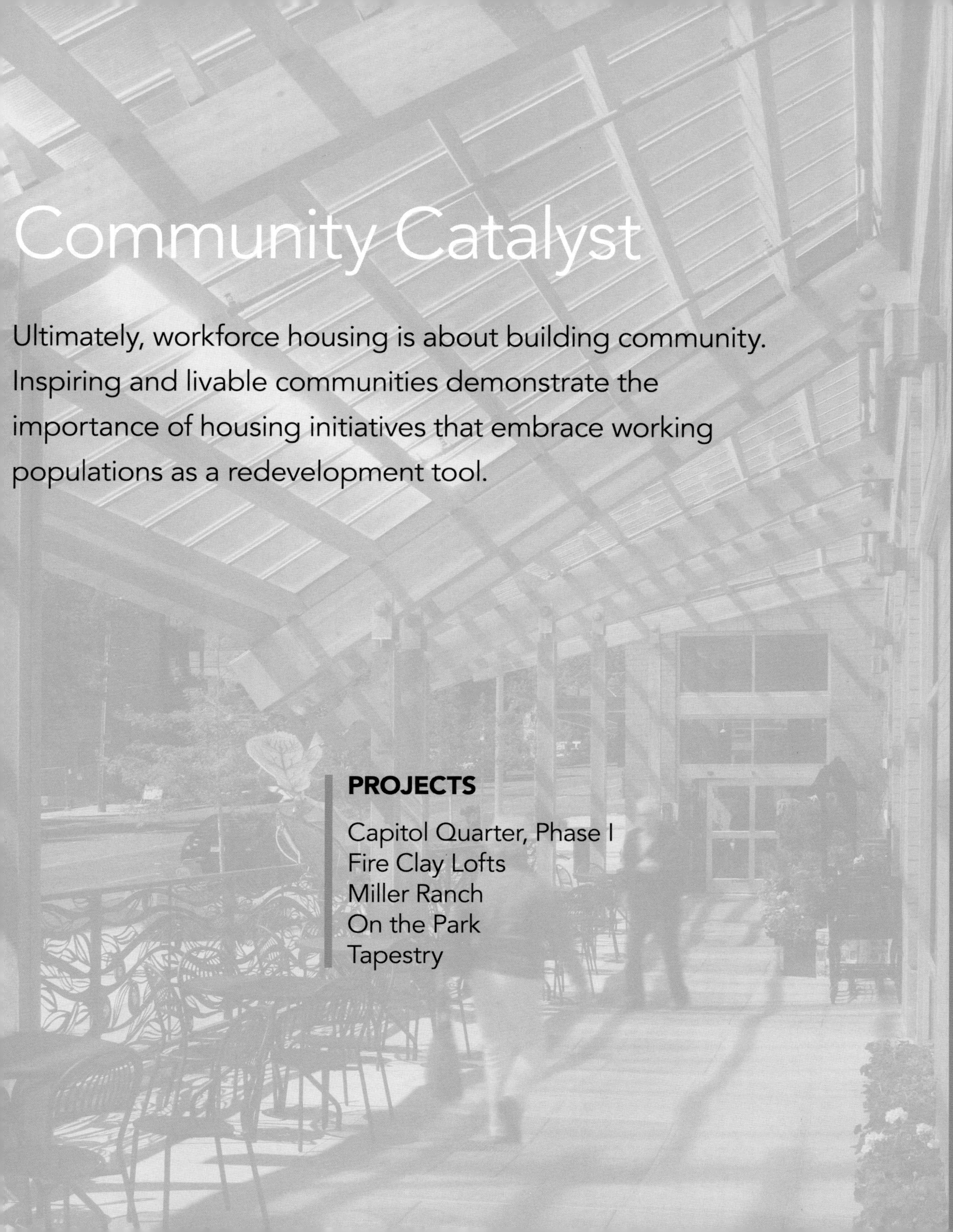

Community Catalyst

Ultimately, workforce housing is about building community. Inspiring and livable communities demonstrate the importance of housing initiatives that embrace working populations as a redevelopment tool.

PROJECTS

Capitol Quarter, Phase I
Fire Clay Lofts
Miller Ranch
On the Park
Tapestry

"We truly tried to integrate the incomes and ownership types—both rental and for-sale—throughout the project."

—Brian Jackson

Capitol Quarter, Phase I

Washington, D.C.

Capitol Quarter is an eight-acre residential component of the 23-acre Capper/Carrollsburg HOPE VI Redevelopment Project—a redevelopment plan that aims to transform blighted public housing into a vibrant mixed-income, mixed-use community in Washington, D.C.

PROJECT DATA

Developers
EYA LLC
Bethesda, Maryland
www.eya.com

Capper/Carrollsburg Ventures
Washington, D.C.

Public Partner
District of Columbia Housing Authority
Washington, D.C.
www.dchousing.org

Design Architect
Lessard Group
Vienna, Virginia
www.lessardgroup.com

Master Planner
Torti Gallas and Partners
Silver Spring, Maryland
www.tortigallas.com

Housing Information
Total number of units: 160
Workforce for-sale units: 36
Affordable rental units: 39
Affordable purchase units: 8
Market-rate units: 77

Occupancy Rate of Workforce Units: 100% anticipated by October 2012

Project Affordability
$295,000–$585,000

Area Median Income, 2011–2012
60% $63,660
100% $106,100
120% $127,320

Development Cost
$55 million

Development Timeline
Date acquired: May 2008
Date started: May 2008
Date sales opened: May 2006 (presales)
Date completed: May 2010

The Capitol Quarter residential development, which includes a mix of market-rate and workforce for-sale townhouses as well as affordable rental units, is designed to blend into the surrounding neighborhoods and meets LEED for Homes standards. Developed by EYA—a Washington-area developer and homebuilder that specializes in urban infill housing—Capitol Quarter will be developed in two phases. When complete, it will include a total of 323 residential units. The first phase of the development was completed in May 2010 with 160 units, 36 of which are workforce housing units. The second phase, currently under construction, will include an additional 163 units. The revitalized neighborhood will represent a national model for mixed-income development, workforce housing, and sustainable growth.

THE PROBLEM

The site, previously home to two public housing complexes—the Arthur Capper and Carrollsburg Dwellings (Arthur Capper/Carrollsburg) in the southeast quadrant of Washington, D.C.—was blighted and severely deteriorated. Built in the 1940s, the public housing complexes consisted of 707 units that were in extreme disrepair and had become economically and functionally obsolete. The neighborhood in which they stood had also fallen into disrepair. Separated from the greater Capitol Hill neighborhood by the Southeast/Southwest Freeway and dominated by light industrial uses, the area was underused, save for public housing and the Washington Navy Yard, a ceremonial and administrative center for the U.S. Navy.

In October 2001, the District of Columbia Housing Authority (DCHA) received a $34.9 million HOPE VI grant from the U.S. Department of Housing and Urban Development for the revitalization of the Arthur Capper/Carrollsburg site. Although the grant was substantial, that amount alone would be insufficient to replace the public housing units being demolished. Using a conservative estimate of $100,000 per unit, total replacement would require more than $70 million—roughly twice the grant amount. Therefore, the ability to leverage other public and private resources was necessary.

THE SOLUTION

In the intervening decade since the HOPE VI grant was awarded, the area has seen extensive investment from both public and private sources. In addition, Nationals Park baseball stadium, the U.S. Department of Transportation office complex, and hundreds of thousands of square feet of additional office space have already been developed. Even with so much new investment, however, this area of the city still lacked population density and, more important, the feel of community: people came to work or to see a baseball game, but few lived there.

With the value of the city-owned land and the perception of the neighborhood being on the rise, the DCHA was able to attract additional private and public investors. The initial HOPE VI grant grew to more than $750 million to form one of the largest urban redevelopment plans in the country. At completion, it would consist of 1,645 residential units, 700,000 square feet of office space, 51,000 square feet of retail space, and an 18,000-square-foot community center. EYA was one of the early partners that could offer regional expertise and private funding sources. Capitol Quarter was designed to bring a diverse group of residents back to this southeast Washington neighborhood. As the first residential project to be completed, Capitol Quarter represents the leading edge of the larger 23-acre planned development.

What was once a concentration of nine city blocks of dilapidated, low-rise public housing is now an 8.8-acre, mixed-income community in a burgeoning Capitol Hill neighborhood. EYA financed the project through a combination of the HOPE VI grant, city subsidies, public infrastructure PILOT (payment in lieu of taxes) bonds, and traditional new-home construction debt/equity financing. The sales of the market-rate units—a highly desirable product in a strong housing market—provided a significant subsidy for the workforce and affordable units, which make up more than half the total units. The result—a mix of market-rate townhouses, affordable workforce residences, and affordable rental apartments—is a sustainable, diverse community for the rapidly redeveloping area of southeast Washington, D.C.

THE PRODUCT

Capitol Quarter is the townhouse component of the larger Capper/Carrollsburg HOPE VI Redevelopment Project. The townhouses range from two to four bedrooms (1,073 to 1,959 square feet) on three levels, with rear-accessed garage parking. The market-rate homes offer similar configurations, with optional fourth levels and upgraded amenities. The average sales price for the workforce units is $361,250; for the market-rate homes, it is $750,000.

Homes at Capitol Quarter are designed to replicate the character of historic Washington, D.C., residences so that the development blends seamlessly into the greater Capitol Hill neighborhood.

Units are tall and narrow, squarely facing the sidewalk, with small frontyards and raised stoops. Facades are natural red brick or pastel-painted brick punctuated by tall, narrow double-hung windows similar to those used in the early 20th-century homes of the area. There is no visible distinction between the market-rate and workforce townhouses, and even the rental flats mimic traditional rowhouse typologies: a typical block will appear from the street to contain nine rowhouses, when in fact it houses four one-level flats, two duplex units, and five townhouses. This careful design was also key to the financing, since the blending of units "helps create value in the mind of the market-rate buyer," according to Brian Jackson, senior vice president at EYA.

In addition to mixing units and blending into the surrounding community, homes at Capitol Quarter are environmentally friendly. Through low-emittance windows, low-flow toilets and faucets, and the use of recycled construction materials, EYA was able to obtain LEED for Homes certification for the residential project. Site-specific factors—an infill location and proximity to public transit, offices, shopping, and recreational options, along with a density of 37 units per acre—add to the project's considerable sustainability cachet.

CONCLUSION
Capitol Quarter represents one of the first steps toward the creation of a vibrant and integrated residential community for a reemerging area of Washington, D.C. The redevelopment will serve as the residential heart connecting the commercial/entertainment district surrounding Nationals Park baseball stadium with the established neighborhood of Capitol

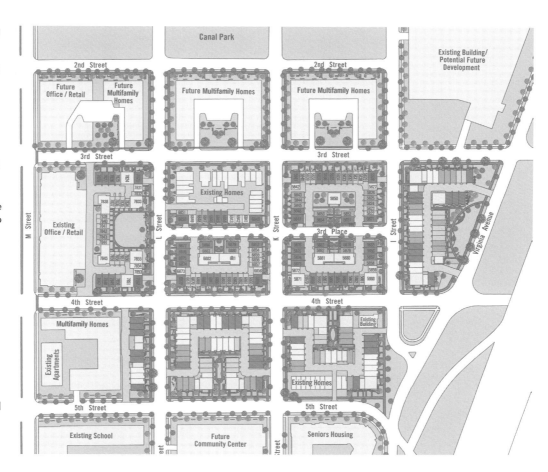

Hill to the north. Although much of the redevelopment is currently under way, this area of the city—for so long forgotten and underused—will become a vibrant part of the city.

Lessons from Industry Leaders

Brian Jackson, Senior Vice President
EYA
Bethesda, Maryland

RICHARD ROSAN: Tell me about EYA.

BRIAN JACKSON: I've been told that five years ago, we were a 100 percent market-rate developer and now we're a 65–70 percent market-rate developer. We are also completely vertically integrated from the entitlement and acquisition side through development and construction to sales and mortgage services—the whole thing. That gives

you a sense of where our projects have been. That's EYA.

ROSAN: Could you describe Capitol Quarter?

JACKSON: The project is located about six blocks southeast of the U.S. Capitol. We are at the center of Eastern Market, the Capitol, the Marine Barracks [Eighth and I streets], and the Anacostia River and not far from the new baseball stadium. The location is actually an important element of the financeability of the project. This project was a reality before baseball agreed to come back to D.C.—proximity to the neighborhood of Capitol Hill and the river really made this project viable.

ROSAN: I understand the project is part of a larger city redevelopment effort.

JACKSON: Yes, Capitol Quarter is a small component of a much larger project. Urban Atlantic, in agreement with the DCHA, is leading the development of the entire 23-acre area. In 2001, it started with a HOPE VI grant of $34.9 million. In total, it is a replacement of 707 public housing units that were scattered throughout the project area. Replacing them will be more than 1,600 residential units: approximately one-third market rate, one-third workforce housing, and one-third public housing. In this case, workforce is defined broadly, going from 50 percent to 115 percent of AMI [area median income] in a homeownership form. Included are a 700,000-square-foot office component, a retail component, and a community center. It is a very large project.

EYA's component is Capitol Quarter, which includes nine blocks of rowhouses. It comprises 323 units across two

phases—the first phase is 160 units. That breaks down to 137 market-rate units, 75 workforce housing units (80–115 percent of AMI), 25 HCVP [Housing Choice Voucher Program] ownership units (50–80 percent of AMI), and 86 affordable rental housing units that provide one-for-one replacements for units lost to demolition.

ROSAN: Describe the architecture.

JACKSON: The architecture is a townhouse style. We truly tried to integrate the incomes and ownership types—both rental and for-sale— throughout the project. Flats look like townhouses, and all units have the same exterior materials. Obviously, we try to make it so there is no distinction from the street as you walk through the community. That was another key to the financing of the project because that helps create the value in the mind of the market-rate buyer. Part of what we are doing is using market-rate land to subsidize the development of affordable housing.

ROSAN: So it is important that buyers feel like they are in a market-rate community?

JACKSON: Yes, EYA as a company believes that approach has helped us be successful in these types of products. We are first and foremost a market-rate developer. So what we are doing is starting with a market-rate concept and then working backward, seeing what we need to do to make the affordable element work within the scope of a viable market-rate community, as opposed to taking an affordable community and trying to add market-rate sales to generate a little cash flow.

ROSAN: The residences are mixed from a physical standpoint. But is the community truly integrated?

JACKSON: Making sure that all the residents are interacting and not clustering is an issue. One of our issues when doing communities that mix rental and for-sale housing is that the owners get together in the homeowners association and make decisions about the community that obviously exclude all tenants. That does not work. You cannot have an association where one-third of the residents are not involved. So we now have gone to a community association model, where certain rights are directly reserved for the owners, such as granting easements and setting budgets, but everyone can get together about how to govern the community and talk about issues.

ROSAN: How were the workforce units incorporated into the development plan?

JACKSON: The sale of the market-rate land—the land underneath the market-rate townhouses—that cash helped build all the affordable housing as well as the workforce housing. In addition, 4 percent Low-Income Housing Tax Credits helped finance the affordable rental housing. Tax-exempt bond financing and PILOT bond financing from D.C. are a significant source of subsidy for this project.

About $6 million in public infrastructure work, including separation of sewers, improvements of curbs and sidewalks, and street trees and lights, has been provided by D.C. as a subsidy. The future homeowners will pay for all that through the use of PILOT bonds, which are basically revenue anticipation bonds on the taxes of the future homeowners as well as the commercial component. There is traditional debt financing as well as traditional equity financing for the market-rate and workforce construction costs.

ROSAN: Are there are any other interesting features of the partnership between EYA and the housing authority?

JACKSON: There is profit participation with the DCHA on the sale of the market-rate units. The DCHA is bringing the land to make the project possible, and so it participates on the additional land sales on a profit participation basis, and that really helps align interests between the development team and the DCHA. So we're on the same page marching toward the same goal.

ROSAN: How do you ensure that the workforce units remain affordable?

JACKSON: We released the first tranche of workforce housing units in 2006. We released 18 units at below-market prices. The affordability control was a price subsidy program with a clawback provision that was controlled by a covenant written by the DCHA. We qualified incomes based on household size and then placed restrictions on resale and added the ten-year covenant to claw back any gain on sale. We priced these units between $295,000 and $395,000. The median income in this area is $100,000, just to give you an idea.

In 2006, we wanted to keep buyers in the city. We are very concerned about price because affordability was getting wildly out of hand. We were trying to keep prices as close to a three-to-one AMI price ratio as possible. We were trying to achieve this delicate balance:

attracting people to the city and making it a real economic opportunity in terms of appreciation but also protecting the affordability. I won't say that we got it right. Also from the DCHA's perspective, it was an important goal to transition former affordable residences to workforce housing. So we had to balance that.

Consequently, we had a lottery because there was too much demand; 147 people had qualified and all 18 units were sold. The median income was under $60,000. We felt like we were achieving what we wanted to achieve.

ROSAN: How does the second dispersal of workforce units differ from the first?

JACKSON: We held another lottery a month ago for the second tranche. The program is designed differently, with the units priced at market rate with a second trust mortgage provided by the DCHA. That second trust subsidizes the market price, holding it down to something that is affordable to the buyer with an income around the AMI. The trust is a 30-year no-interest nonamortizing loan that is due on sale or refinancing.

One of the issues with the first program that we tried to address with the second tranche was the concern about the absolute difference in price between a market-rate townhouse (which was selling for at least $600,000) and a workforce house (selling for about $350,000). It's essentially the same house, minus some features on the interior. And so part of the decision of the DCHA and the development team was to use a program with a nominal price that was more in line with the true market value of a home. The DCHA would be protected through the second

trust rather than through a clawback provision. The cash price could be brought down to what was affordable. There are multiple ways to do it. I'm not saying this is the right way to do it either. But it is an interesting experiment when you have two workforce housing programs running simultaneously. We'll see which works better.

ROSAN: The market-rate sales are essential to the mixed-income nature of the project. How do you ensure market-rate buyers will be interested in the product?

JACKSON: One thing we figured out from another project on which we partnered with Urban Atlantic in Alexandria was that market-rate buyers will purchase in these mixed-income communities if the amenities and features of the home are up to their expectations. There is a big difference between the interior of a workforce unit and a market-rate unit. There is a 10 percent difference in the development costs of the two units, which is attributable almost entirely to the costs of the units' interior.

We also found that fee-simple ownership has a strong appeal. For the market-rate buyers, there is a higher value. We found out this appeal works on the tax-credit side too. Everyone owns their own lot. Even the stacked affordable rental units are actually on individual lots. So from a tax-credit perspective, you are not actually investing in a mixed-income property; you are buying your own property, and that was a significant issue.

ROSAN: If you could pick one element, what was the key to making this project work?

unaffordable to many would not happen at Fire Clay Lofts.

The four-acre mixed-use redevelopment combines the adaptive use of an old warehouse with new construction to create 166 condominiums, including 32 affordable residences. A total of 14 buildings featuring units in flat, loft, townhouse, and live/work configurations are located on the streetfront and perimeter of the two-block site.

THE PRODUCT

Fire Clay Lofts is located on Blake Street between 30th and 33rd Streets, a few blocks northeast of Lower Downtown and Coors Field (the project borders stadium parking). The site lies in a busy industrial neighborhood with a mix of old factories and warehouses, salvage yards, and even a junkyard for double-decker buses. When the project began in 2000, the neighborhood had relatively few and dispersed residents, with the exception of those residing in a live/work artists' community, Silver Square, located next to the site.

The four-acre site has a rich industrial history going back more than a century. Fire Clay Lofts is named for the Fire Clay Brick Company, located on the site for more than 100 years. The business ceased its manufacturing operations in the 1970s; one of the two remaining structures experienced a fire and collapsed, leaving the Cable Building as the only structure that the developer was able to reuse.

The Cable Building and 13 new structures are connected by walkways, courtyards, and open space. Many of the structures are sited along the eastern and western streetfront perimeters: the site design defines its edges with buildings and

parking, creating courtyards and other interior spaces where residents can meet and mingle. "We were so much freer to experiment with design and materials because of the eclectic neighborhood we were in," says Susan Powers, president of Urban Ventures LLC. "That was an opportunity for us, rather than a problem, and we embraced it."

CONCLUSION

At the time, the influence of Denver's affluent and lively LoDo district had not yet spread to the neighborhood, which was relatively isolated. Local residents wanted affordable homeownership opportunities and did not want land values to increase to the point where they could not afford to live there. The development team held a series of open houses and meetings with a buildout model of the project and through these meetings became attuned to the community's desire for a balance between high-quality construction and maintaining a diverse neighborhood.

The local community group, composed of business owners and residents, wanted residential development with mixed uses and mixed incomes, live/work opportunities, and good-quality construction and supported the project throughout the planning, zoning, and construction process. Since the project broke ground, several mixed-use residential developments have opened along Blake Street and in surrounding areas, adding several hundred more residential units to the neighborhood.

Lessons from Industry Leaders

Susan Powers, President
Urban Ventures LLC
Denver, Colorado

RICHARD ROSAN: Let's talk about this neighborhood.

SUSAN POWERS: I think what attracted me to the area is it's on the edge of downtown Denver, but it has its own character. It's really an industrial area that's in transition. So Fire Clay Lofts was one of the first residential uses developed there. I was attracted to the notion of being a kind of pioneer in that neighborhood and being able to experiment with architecture and materials and with everything else we would want to experiment with because we weren't sitting in the middle of an established residential neighborhood that had a lot going on. And the residents that happened to be in the neighborhood and businesses that were pro-development said, "Come in here and do this."

ROSAN: You sort of had a clean slate.

POWERS: We did; it was very unusual.

ROSAN: How many years ago was this?

POWERS: We bought the property 11 years ago. I think we learned over time—because we phased it; because the economy made us phase it—that everything takes longer than you expect. But we were able to change the product we were building as the economy changed and meet different needs. And we were able to incorporate the things that we learned into each phase, such as sizing the units and mixing units, as we went on.

ROSAN: So when you started, your concept was to build mixed-income housing.

POWERS: Right. It was always to build mixed income; it is a for-sale project. And 20 percent of the units are deed restricted. It was just as much a philosophical perspective that our company has to build communities and to continue to have that as part of our mission, making housing available to people that could otherwise not afford to live downtown.

ROSAN: So you made it deed restricted?

POWERS: Yes, we made it deed restricted.

ROSAN: And the other 80 are market rate?

POWERS: Right. But because the area the project is in never had the inflation or deflation in values, it's been a much more stable area than other parts of the city or, certainly, in the country in that respect, over the last couple of years.

ROSAN: How did you make the 20 percent deed-restricted units less expensive?

POWERS: Well, you know, there's always an argument about whether you can— you can't raise the prices above the market anyway. So I think we were really conscious of costs overall. We have two great architects involved who were very cost conscious and had designed a lot of affordable housing. And we lucked out with contractors that also understood the mission and were very careful. So we just kept the costs down.

ROSAN: You bought the land reasonably.

POWERS: We certainly did. I don't know how this will compare with other places in the country, but the land was $17 a square foot. We had to do

environmental cleanup just because of the nature of the property.

ROSAN: Did you have grants to help you?

POWERS: We got one grant from the city: a home loan of $309,000, which converted to a grant once we built and sold the last affordable unit. So it was in place as a covenant on the property. Then the city released it at the end.

ROSAN: And the land cost total was what?

POWERS: $3.5 million.

ROSAN: So you got 10 percent of the land cost back.

POWERS: Right. And then the total project cost, I think, was $48 million.

ROSAN: For how many units?

POWERS: One hundred and sixty-six. They're spread out over two city blocks. So it's not 166 units in a high rise, which would be a different kind of building, which wouldn't take up as much land. But the density is something like 32 units to the acre.

ROSAN: You didn't get a zoning bonus?

POWERS: No, and I think we built as much as was appropriate for the neighborhood or for the market.

ROSAN: The market for the market-rate housing is still probably below other areas in Denver, correct?

POWERS: Yes, it's definitely below that for downtown, but it's enough on a per-square-foot basis; it's

certainly competitive with many of the neighborhoods.

ROSAN: What did it sell for?

POWERS: In general, they were about $300 a square foot. But you know, Denver numbers are not San Francisco or New York or Boston numbers. So at the height of the market downtown, they were creeping up toward $500 a square foot, but they were mostly around $400. So they held their value, which is important.

ROSAN: You sold the 20 percent deed-restricted units?

POWERS: Yes, and we had no problems selling any of them. In fact, they were the first ones to sell.

ROSAN: And what price per square foot did they go for?

POWERS: They were probably closer to $220 a square foot. So an affordable unit would have sold for about $160,000 and a market-rate unit would have sold for $220,000. That was kind of the difference there. The finishes between the units didn't differ significantly, so you really couldn't tell that much of a difference between them. We did have upgrades available. And I think we probably put in some upgrades in the market-rate units, such as more hardwood flooring. But in general, they looked alike.

This development occurred before the city had an Inclusionary Housing Ordinance in place. It was kind of the evolution, because the city was struggling with how to create more affordability and everything was being negotiated on a case-by-case basis before the Inclusionary Housing

Ordinance went into effect. When that happened, the city gave a $5,000 bonus for each unit. But we weren't eligible because the ordinance wasn't in place at the time. But I guess the difference in the market—which was so much stronger at that time—made enough of a difference in what we were charging to make up for this gap.

ROSAN: Of all the projects that we looked at, you are unique in that your subsidy was so low. But you had a combination of inexpensive land, the one grant from the city, and you were cost conscious.

POWERS: And being low-rise helps. Only the last building had an elevator. We hit the market in phases and got great pricing. This last phase ended up being something like $106 a square foot. And the renovation of the building was $88 a square foot. So we hit it just right. And, you know, a 10 percent increase in those costs would have knocked us out. So we were fortunate.

ROSAN: What about sustainability features?

POWERS: It wasn't called that back then. But our architect, Tim Van Meter, was very conscious of sustainability, especially in the first phase. He had moved here from San Francisco where they were ahead of the game. We used bamboo flooring, which we actually bought directly from a plant in China. It came off a boat, went to Los Angeles, and was delivered by train about six blocks from where we were. This effort was more hands-on than we expected.

And we've used Aquatherm heating systems. We've also incorporated a lot of things—we never went through a process of establishing LEED—there wasn't anything called LEED at the time. But we advertised the project, marketed it, and pointed out the materials we were using. We used cement board that, we felt, was environmentally responsible.

ROSAN: Did you use Energy Star appliances and things like that?

POWERS: Yes, we did. We were making up the rules as we went. But it was important for the kinds of people who were attracted there, not just because they were cost conscious but because they were environmentally conscious too.

ROSAN: You have some nice open space behind some of the units—private and public.

POWERS: We do. We have a whole row of townhouses behind the main buildings that have backyards with great views of the mountains. And then we have some common areas and common vegetable gardens that the community has developed.

ROSAN: What about other amenities?

POWERS: One way we saved money on the building was by not including a lot of amenities. There's a gym two blocks away that everybody belongs to. People have been fine with that. They've all said that's where they go to socialize as well. So it has not been an issue. And when we look at the people who purchased the deed-restricted units especially, we have exactly who we would want to have live there. We have a lot of teachers and we have several police officers.

ROSAN: What does the deed restriction say if they sell their unit?

POWERS: They can get up to 3 percent a year in appreciation. And they have to sell to somebody who has an income that qualifies as well. It's a recorded deed. And when they sell, the title company will pull up the records.

ROSAN: When you first started, of course, the economy was so different, but what downpayments were required?

POWERS: Most people were buying these units with FHA [Federal Housing Administration] loans, so they had 3 percent down. And on the market-rate units, we required 5 percent. Today, it would be much more.

ROSAN: Was the development process difficult?

POWERS: No. We did rezone the property because it was all zoned industrial, so we rezoned it residential.

ROSAN: Did you buy the property before rezoning or did you just have an option on it?

POWERS: We were under contract, and we waited until we were pretty close. We were pretty much through the process and knew we didn't have any barriers there.

ROSAN: Did you have any kind of design review by the city?

POWERS: We did. And I think it was probably a challenge for them because it was not a normal project—it wasn't a neighborhood that had a context, particularly.

ROSAN: So when they rezoned it, they mandated a design process?

THE PRODUCT

Miller Ranch is a community-oriented neighborhood with 282 homes: 69 single-family homes, 64 duplexes, 49 rowhouses, and 100 condominiums across 31 acres of land. The density achieved is approximately ten dwelling units per acre. Prices run 30 to 50 percent below market rate, and the homes must be purchased by local residents or by qualified buyers who are employed within Eagle County, with preference given to those who are employed within the town of Vail.

The project density helped achieve development cost efficiency by using new urbanist principles and design. All units within the development are workforce housing units, but a wide range of housing types were made available to accommodate different household sizes at varying income levels. Single-family detached homes make up almost 50 percent of the total housing units. Homes range in size from one to four bedrooms, with the majority being two- and three-bedroom units. The development is designed in a traditional grid street pattern with alley-accessed garages—high-density design not normally seen in Eagle County. By clustering units, over 40 acres of riverfront open space were preserved.

The project includes several amenities and public benefits, such as schools, open space, and recreation facilities. The transportation network was also improved by adding roads, bridges, transit stops, and a regional bike path.

CONCLUSION

One of the most outstanding aspects of Miller Ranch is its role as a catalyst for the redevelopment of Edwards. The project now includes several

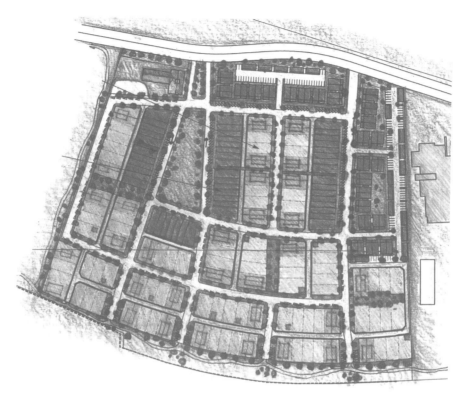

schools, a community center, a child care facility, a multitude of parks and recreation facilities, and a sheriff's office substation. The implementation of new urbanist principles through a mix of housing types, interconnected street grid networks, increased density, and walkable design created an integrated residential project, blending into its surroundings seamlessly. The pedestrian-friendly streets allow residents to use multimodal transportation and enjoy a walk through the park or a bike ride to downtown Edwards. The community has quickly evolved into one of the most desirable neighborhoods in the entire region.

Lessons from Industry Leaders

Don Cohen, Executive Director
Economic Council of Eagle County
Eagle, Colorado

Alex Potente, Director of Housing and Development
Eagle County Department of Housing and Development
Eagle, Colorado

RICHARD ROSAN: Can you tell me about the history of Miller Ranch?

DON COHEN: Miller Ranch was conceived at a time when real estate values seemed to be relentlessly going up and nobody was really thinking about what would happen if real estate values went down. The county acquired this land in the 1990s. So this project was around for a long time before the commissioners and the county actually took it up. The county helped facilitate a couple of intergovernmental agreements with the school district and the town.

ROSAN: Where was the leadership for this project?

COHEN: The county and the town of Vail.

ALEX POTENTE: The county put in the land. We split the profits with the developer. We did get some repayment from the sale of units. ASW Realty helped shape what the project would look like, and it was an advantage for the project that the architecture is quite good.

ROSAN: Can you talk more about the planning process?

POTENTE: There was an Edwards subarea master plan and an Eagle County area plan, both of which had to be consistent. But largely, the details of the plan were hashed out at the entitlement process, which is the process the developer led the county through after we selected the developer.

COHEN: There was no zoning on the property. It was originally part of this Berry Creek subdivision called Single Tree, on the other side of the freeway. So we actually ceded some of the water rights back into this area, but it was still a ranch.

ROSAN: What is the median income in the area?

POTENTE: Area median income for a family of four is about $83,000 a year. So it's a substantial income, but not the high-middle or high incomes that the second-home market targets.

ROSAN: What's the median home price in the area?

POTENTE: For a single-family home, it is about $800,000. So the county had the land set up, attracted developers, selected ASW Realty, then tranche

by tranche added the land into the partnership, and the land would then be developed. In between, the land was entitled as a whole.

ROSAN: So the developer looked at the cost to develop these buildings with free land and came up with a number that was going to work?

COHEN: Right. Our prior county manager tried to calculate the cost of the subsidy per unit. It was always hotly debated, but that number seemed to be $50,000 per unit. So basically the county put in about a $15 million commitment. Part of that cost included some of the infrastructure improvements needed for the project.

ROSAN: How were the schools and other amenities developed?

POTENTE: The residential development at Miller Ranch really grounded a lot of the other projects: the high school, the grade school, the community fitness facility, and the community center. They were all built after we completed the residential construction.

ROSAN: Did you pay a premium for high-quality architecture?

POTENTE: I don't think we paid a premium. We just luckily chose a good architect, and we had a good contractor.

ROSAN: When you designed this project in the early 2000s, were you thinking as much about green design as we do now?

POTENTE: Not as much. Although I think it turned out that there are many new urbanist elements that make the development fairly green in nature.

"We're not just providing bricks and sticks. We're trying to create a community and fit into the overall neighborhood."

—Mike Gruber

On the Park

Seattle, Washington

On the Park is a high-quality mixed-use redevelopment located five miles northwest of Seattle's business district in the emerging Ballard neighborhood.

PROJECT DATA

Developer
Security Properties
Seattle, Washington

Partners
City of Seattle

AFL-CIO Building Investment Trust
www.aflcio-bit.com

Design Architect
Bumgardner Architects
Seattle, Washington
www.bumgardner.biz

Housing Information
Total number of units: 268
Workforce rental units: 54
Market-rate rental units: 214

Occupancy Rate of Workforce Units: 100%

Project Affordability

	Workforce	Market Rate
Studios	$1,199	$1,150–$1,730
One-bedrooms	$1,370	$1,395–$3,090
Two-bedrooms	$1,734	$2,062–$3,595

Area Median Income, 2011–2012

60%	$49,020
100%	$81,700
120%	$98,040

Development Cost
$86.7 million

Development Timeline

Date acquired:	August 2003
Date started:	December 2007
Date rentals opened:	March 2010
Date completed:	May 2010

With a rich history rooted in Seattle's maritime and lumber industries, the Ballard neighborhood has undergone significant revitalization in recent years as one of the city's target areas for high-density development to help reduce urban sprawl.

On the Park is literally "on the park," sharing a property line with the city's Ballard Commons Park in an ideal transition from Ballard's town center activities and services to a quieter, more

residential feel. Located on an urban infill site that spans 1.5 acres, On the Park includes 268 apartments (54 of which are income restricted), in a mix of styles and sizes to accommodate a range of household types and incomes. The building addresses sustainability with energy-efficient building systems and a walkable neighborhood with excellent transit access—one bus stop is on the west side of the property and two others are two blocks away, providing daily service to Seattle's central business district and other locations throughout the city.

THE PROBLEM

As the largest city in the Pacific Northwest, Seattle is home to a range of employment sectors, notably many internet and technology companies, including software giant Microsoft. Employment opportunities along with an interesting culture make Seattle a highly desirable city for younger workers, many with modest incomes. Between 2000 and 2010, the city of Seattle's population increased by 8 percent to 608,660. The metro area has a population of 3.4 million, making it the 15th largest in the United States.

Because of its geographic location, developable land in Seattle is limited, which drives up costs. These constraints, along with strong population growth, create an expensive housing market. Seattle also has a high proportion of renter households—53 percent, compared with a national average of 34 percent.

THE SOLUTION

On the Park employed several strategies to achieve its goal of offering 20 percent of its units as workforce housing. Partnering with the city of Seattle to participate

in the city's multifamily tax exemption program provided property tax abatements on the residential portion of the building for 12 years in exchange for setting aside at least 20 percent of the units for households earning at or below 90 percent of the area median income (AMI). The developer was able to offer rents that include all basic utilities: gas, water, sewer, and trash removal. Typical of Seattle, the units are not air conditioned.

Local zoning regulations allowed greater density for urban mixed-use projects. The project is part of the Ballard Municipal Center Master Plan area, which allows density bonuses in exchange for community benefits. In this case, a height bonus of one level was provided in exchange for building townhouses along the park with upper floors set back from the park. The developer also partnered with the AFL-CIO Building Investment Trust (BIT), which financed the project. BIT is a pension fund that invests in construction projects in supply-constrained urban markets. BIT's combined goals are creating union jobs, investing in urban development, and providing solid returns for pension plan participants.

THE PRODUCT

On the Park represents a striking transformation from an aging grocery store with a surface parking lot to a thriving, mixed-use, mixed-income, multifamily housing community—all in the context of a broader neighborhood revitalization that completes the vision of the city's master plan for the Ballard neighborhood. The development is an eight-story building with a 45,000-square-foot grocery store, a small retail space, and the leasing office for the apartments on the ground level.

Two levels of underground parking are available for the grocery store and for residents (for a fee). Of the 268 apartments, 54 (20 percent) are workforce units affordable to residents earning up to 90 percent of AMI ($73,500). Workforce units include 14 studios, 28 one-bedroom units, and 12 two-bedroom units. Market-rate units include 55 studios, 111 one-bedroom units, and 48 two-bedroom units.

The developer's focus was to create a property that would offer an excellent quality of life for its residents by creating an interactive pedestrian-friendly experience around all perimeters of the building. On the western and commercial sides, the facades are replete with commissioned art installations. To the east, townhouse terraces directly greet Ballard Commons Park. Townhouses continue around the corner to the north side, their entry stoops extending the residential scale and character of the neighborhood. On the south side, seven floors of flats surround a second-story 10,000-square-foot landscaped courtyard and amenity space, which also provides natural light and views for units facing the courtyard. In addition to the outstanding location and accessibility, the building features top-notch architecture and attractive amenities. Due to careful planning, nearly every unit has a water or mountain view. Other amenities include a clubhouse, fitness center, theater, outdoor spa, and barbecue pavilion. The clean, modern design of the building is enhanced throughout with works of art by regional artists.

The development incorporates green construction and sustainable land use practices. By redeveloping an underused site, On the Park is breathing new life into the site and demonstrating the benefits of efficient land use by leveraging existing infrastructure and accommodating urban growth patterns. All waste materials generated during the demolition and construction phase were recycled. Innovative building technologies were employed not only to reduce costs but also to enhance the project's quality. On the Park represents one of the first projects in the city to be designed and constructed using a propriety structural system. The wall systems and compressed composite floor assembly allowed more floors to be built over the concrete structure than would have been allowed with wood framing or traditional steel framing. The proprietary panels were manufactured off site, which provided a number of additional benefits, including greater quality control, faster construction timelines, and straighter metal panels when compared with wood framing, allowing for higher-quality wall finish levels. In addition, the manufactured wall panels incorporate resilient channel and sound isolators that further improve the tenant's experience in the building.

CONCLUSION

Despite Seattle's experience during the economic downturn, On the Park's market acceptance is particularly noteworthy with more than 90 percent of the units already rented. In a city where growth outpaces the availability of affordable rental units, On the Park provides 54 units affordable to moderate-income households. Through innovative design and thoughtful amenities, On the Park is a development that offers a high quality of life for all its residents. The workforce units were made possible by using a number of strategies, including creative financing and incentives such as a height bonus.

From a community standpoint, On the Park redeveloped an underused site that held a small grocery store and surface parking. The redevelopment more than doubled the size of the grocery store (which kept the employees from the old store), while adding a substantial and highly attractive mixed-income residential component. In fact, On the Park has proved that the right vision can produce followers and inspire others. The development serves as a model for sustainable urban redevelopment and has become a development multiplier; inspiring the introduction of new condominiums, apartments, restaurants, and retail amenities, which continue to open in proximity to the development and add vitality to the area.

Lessons from Industry Leaders

Mike Gruber, Director of Development
Security Properties
Seattle, Washington

Ivone Mendoza, Resident Manager
Madrona Ridge Residential
Seattle, Washington

RICHARD ROSAN: Tell me about this neighborhood.

MIKE GRUBER: It has a Scandinavian history, so it used to be geared pretty heavily toward fishing. The ship canal is due south of us by just a couple of blocks. And there are some wonderful old shops. The neighborhood is the best of past and new. People have taken some of the old storefronts and created all sorts of entertainment venues. It's one of the most bustling areas in Seattle now. With technology jobs and the rest, this area has become a magnet for people from all over the globe.

ROSAN: And the building? Describe the construction.

GRUBER: The structure is unique and proprietary to the engineering firm that designed it. It's light-gauge steel frame with concrete on a pan deck. It uses a lightweight concrete, and it allowed us to have more floors than would have been possible with wood framing. It's the first project we've done this way.

The green element of that light-gauge metal framing is that it's often recycled steel. And the windows are some of the biggest you'll find around here. We're drawing natural light. So on sunny days, you're going to pick up heat gain as well, which is a good thing. A huge benefit of the lightweight framing is that we have no concrete sheer walls penetrating through the QFC Store [the grocery].

ROSAN: Tell me about the mechanical system. Is it centralized?

GRUBER: We have centralized hot water; and for heat, the units have wall heaters—not baseboard but small fan coil units.

ROSAN: I understand MFTE [multifamily property tax exemption] residents don't pay for utilities. How do you do that? Are they all metered separately?

IVONE MENDOZA: The program gives us two ways to do it. Either we charge a little bit lower rent and the resident pays all utilities, or they give us the option to charge a little bit higher rent, and then there's the utility allowance.

ROSAN: And the units are interchangeable? You didn't do anything special in any of them. You didn't use cheaper countertops in the kitchen, for example.

GRUBER: They're identical. I will qualify that on the top floor, we've created more of a penthouse level. Those units have granite counters and nicer plumbing fixtures and appliances. But everything else, all the finish materials are the same.

ROSAN: Who uses the party facility?

MENDOZA: It's open to all the residents, and we reserve it for private events. We also host at least one resident party or function per month. Our last function was two weeks ago. About 160 people showed up.

GRUBER: We're not just providing bricks and sticks. We're trying to create a community and fit into the overall neighborhood. And I think we've been successful in that regard.

ROSAN: What is that interesting thing in the main entrance?

GRUBER: Our architect had an idea here. As you might imagine, we have a number of gray days; so we really wanted to draw in natural light. Early in the conceptual planning, he said, "Maybe we could do a glass stair and a glass bridge." Lo and behold, that's what we've created. Chris Daley, the artist, deserves huge credit.

I'll share another fun story. My guidelines to Chris were, "It needs to look great, but it absolutely needs to work and be safe." Of course, he had to get things certified by an engineer and so on. We asked, "What are we going to do on the sides?" He showed up one day with these big maritime pulleys and said, "I got these out of salvage years ago and always thought I would find some way to use them." So he cut them and created these pieces, came up with these etchings, and used these LEDs to light them.

ROSAN: The artwork is a unique feature of this building.

GRUBER: And it doesn't come for free, so we're always making tradeoffs on what we do. But every amenity is available to every resident, whether the unit is workforce or market rate.

One fun thing is outside. Alexi is an artist we've worked with before. He caught wind that all his artist buddies were doing stuff here and he wasn't. So he kept coming to our office and saying, "I'd really like to be involved." He pitched this idea of creating these benches. The black stone comes from Lummi Island here in the Northwest.

ROSAN: And the seats are white marble . . . very impressive.

GRUBER: The idea was that they're kind of like sailing ships since we are in an area that's maritime. They are kind of queued up like boats in a regatta.

In terms of design, our goal was to create something Scandinavian or Danish modern in feel. The other thing we wanted to do was to create a hub, and our architect really came through. If you want to see everybody, the mail is here, the fitness center, a movie theater, the registration desk—it's a hub for activities. The other thing that sets us apart is this synergy with the street-level grocery store. When we hold activities, they partner with us. So it's been great for them and us.

MENDOZA: Yes, we've had great rapport with the manager of QFC and its employees, and also with the neighborhood. I can't stress enough the amount of time we spend in the neighborhood bringing in the local merchants and vendors to present whatever products they have to our residents. We've had such a great turnout for the events and positive feedback from residents. I actually have local merchants come to me and ask when we are doing the next party. So it's no longer our seeking who's going to be next, it's them coming to us because they know what we have here.

ROSAN: So this is probably unique in the neighborhood. The other buildings don't have these kinds of facilities.

GRUBER: And it's not easily replicated. If a competitor wanted to open across the block, they are not going to be able to get a grocery store in there.

One last thing, there is an organization in Seattle called FareStart that takes people who are homeless, former drug addicts, who have different problems, and puts them to work hopefully to get them back to being productive members of society. They have a restaurant in Seattle; you and I could go there and the food is excellent. They have a culinary program. So one of their lead chefs moved into our building and he is a caterer now. One of his favorite features is our demo kitchen. He comes to our kitchen and does all his food prep here.

With such high quality and the location, people just love it. And the grocery store—imagine living where you have a 24-hour fully stocked pantry right below you. The other thing is the area around Ballard Avenue; it is special. The real proof is can you fill it up with tenants.

ROSAN: I see that you have AFL-CIO financing.

GRUBER: They are our partner, and this is an all-equity deal. This is the other thing—I've got some real passion about this. I think it's the first project we've ever done with union money. I let them know early on that we do a lot of things all over the country, and this would be a kind of litmus test for whether we do this again. PNC is the trustee that managed these funds for the union. But just to circle back, one of the things that I really loved about this is that the kinds of guys who were working to build this place, their pension money helped pay for it.

ROSAN: Is this union built?

GRUBER: It is 100 percent.

ROSAN: You had to do that with the AFL-CIO.

GRUBER: Correct. They were not part of our first discussion. We went to our usual suspects; then things worked out and we ended up using PNC and AFL-CIO money, but what a cool concept.

ROSAN: Of course that's what it was set up to do.

GRUBER: To generate jobs and to actually build housing that their own members could live in. And that was accomplished. And think about when this was built. We broke ground in December 2007. We put a ton of people to work at a time when jobs just started disappearing. And they are the kinds of jobs that everyone is talking about. They've got retirement benefits and they've got health benefits. And the money that this project ultimately throws off will foster retirement returns for them, and so it's just neat the way all these elements came together.

ROSAN: You leased up quickly?

MENDOZA: It took us about 14 months.

ROSAN: Did the workforce units go first?

MENDOZA: No, they actually started a little bit later. We were already open before we started the workforce units, and work did go pretty quickly. In regard to the workforce piece, we have people from the grocery store below that live here, including a cashier. We have four teachers, writers, self-employed or what not. We have retired people and people fresh out of college just starting their life.

ROSAN: It's interesting with the mix of income, but nobody knows where the higher-end units are because some of these people are paying a substantial amount of rent.

MENDOZA: I live in the building and that's been great. With the resident retention and with our parties, we've really created a sense of community. At our last party, we invited 15 people who were waiting to move in to come and meet their neighbors. Amazing. They showed up and interacted, and now they want to bump up their move-in date and move in as soon as possible.

ROSAN: Are there children living here?

MENDOZA: We don't have many, maybe about five younger than 12 or 13. We probably have about three or four teenagers, and that's including my child. We have a lot of singles and young couples and quite a few older folks. I would say that the older folks would be the majority of our penthouse rentals. And they love it here. We have a really great resident profile. Even though we have much older and much younger people, everyone mixes well when we have these functions. Everyone interacts very well together.

GRUBER: Our view on this property— and I think our partner feels the same way—is as a long-term hold. And I think that's something that is important to share.

ROSAN: Because it is a long-term hold, you probably made some design decisions that are more upscale than they might have been otherwise

GRUBER: In terms of the durability of the project and in terms of finishes, we are not a merchant developer. I do believe there is a different mind-set and that it manifests itself in a superior project when you are focused on a longer-term hold.

"One very important lesson we have learned is that income mixing is actually very easy."

—Jonathan Rose

Tapestry

New York, New York

Developed jointly by the Jonathan Rose Companies and Lettire Construction Corporation, Tapestry is a 12-story mixed-income residential building with community-serving ground-floor retail uses.

PROJECT DATA

Developers
Jonathan Rose Companies
New York, New York
www.rose-network.com

Lettire Construction Corporation
New York, New York
www.lettire.com

Public Partners
New York City Department of Housing
Preservation and Development
www.nyc.gov/hpd

New York City Housing Development
Corporation
www.nychdc.com

New York State Energy Research and
Development Authority
http://nyserda.ny.gov

Design Architects
MHG Architects
New York, New York
www.mhgarch.com

Pei Cobb Freed Partners
New York, New York
www.pcf-p.com

Housing Information
Total number of units: 185
Workforce rental units (middle income): 55
Affordable rental units (low income): 37
Market-rate rental units: 93

Occupancy Rate of Workforce Units: 100%

Project Affordability
Rental prices for studio–three bedrooms:
40% AMI $462–$686 (n/a for three bedrooms)
50% AMI $596–$1,002
130% AMI $1,448–$2,729
Market $1,887–$3,683

Area Median Income, 2011–2012
60% $48,120
100% $80,200
120% $96,240

Development Cost
$70 million

Development Timeline
Date acquired: November 2008
Date started: November 2008
Date rentals opened: June 2010
Date completed: May 2010

Case Study

Located in the East Harlem section of New York City, Tapestry is a 219,000-square-foot building that contains 185 units, 55 of which are set aside for middle-income tenants with incomes of 130 percent of the area median income (AMI). The project was developed under New York City's Housing Development Corporation's (HDC's) innovative 50/30/20 program, which encourages mixed-income residential development. The developers of the LEED-Gold building also used grants and loans to design sustainably, including installing energy-efficient systems and "smart" outlets that residents can use to monitor and control electricity usage.

THE PROBLEM

East Harlem is a blend of very low-income households living side by side with moderate- to middle-income households. Market-rate rents in Manhattan remain out of reach for both groups. The challenge for developers has been to create fiscally sustainable buildings that local residents could

afford, giving them the opportunity to remain in a rapidly gentrifying neighborhood while creating a project that appeals to market-rate renters.

The site where Tapestry now stands was once a series of derelict and vacant lots. At the foot of the Robert F. Kennedy Bridge (also known as the Triborough Bridge), the site offered an opportunity to establish a sustainable, mixed-income building at a prominent gateway into Manhattan and to fulfill a vision for the city along one of Harlem's most historic commercial corridors.

THE SOLUTION

The project was able to meet the workforce and affordable housing needs of the community through participation in the HDC's innovative 50/30/20 program. Under the program, the HDC provides low-interest loans to multifamily rental developers in which half the units may be rented at market rates, as long as 20 percent of the apartments are restricted for low-income tenants (40 to 50 percent of AMI) and 30 percent are reserved for workforce housing. The HDC uses the proceeds from the sale of tax-exempt bonds to make first mortgages and uses its corporate reserves to make 1 percent second mortgage loans.

The tax-exempt first mortgage—which covered 60 percent of Tapestry's total development cost—allowed the project's low-income units to qualify for federal Low-Income Housing Tax Credits and its workforce and market-rate units to use "recycled" bonds, which provide a tax-exempt rate. To further support affordability, New York City's Department of Housing Preservation and Development sold five of the nine lots assembled to create Tapestry to the developers for $1 a lot and provided a 20-year tax exemption in exchange for the creation of long-term affordable and middle-income residences. The project also received $500,000 in grants from the New York State Energy Research and Development Authority and Enterprise Community Partners to encourage sustainable development of workforce and affordable housing.

Workforce housing affordability at Tapestry is protected for 35 years through an HDC regulator agreement, recorded as a restrictive covenant against the land. Additionally, as a condition to receiving tax benefits, all units at Tapestry are rent stabilized with annual rent increases for renewals and new leases governed by AMI limits or state guidelines.

THE PRODUCT

The project is located one block from 125th Street, Harlem's main commercial corridor. East Harlem is a dense, urban neighborhood well served by local and regional public transportation options. The site is part of the city's River to River Rezoning Plan for the 125th Street corridor, a multiagency effort to infuse the neighborhood with residential, retail, cultural, and entertainment uses. The development team worked closely with local officials and community members to integrate the project into the River to River Rezoning initiative.

The workforce units rent for between $1,448 for a studio and $2,729 for a three-bedroom apartment. The rent for market-rate units is approximately 20 percent higher. All the units have large bay windows that flood the residences with daylight. The project includes 8,300 square feet of community-serving retail that brings the corner of 124th Street and Second Avenue to life.

Tapestry is Harlem's first LEED-Gold-certified residential mixed-use building, improving energy efficiency by an estimated 20 percent compared with typical multifamily buildings. In partnership with Columbia University, the developer installed "smart" outlets, which allow the tenant to control appliances remotely—turning off or programming a television, for example—and to monitor usage data. The structure, designed by New York–based MHG Architects and Pei Cobb Freed Partners, features a green roof that reduces stormwater runoff, rainwater harvesting that replenishes cooling towers, a highly insulated building envelope, low-flow plumbing fixtures, and Energy Star–rated appliances. The building's terraces have extensive plantings that provide significant outdoor recreational space, and the building has a low-cost gym for residents that encourages a more active lifestyle.

CONCLUSION

The first residents moved into Tapestry in June 2010. The building has remained occupied over 95 percent on average since stabilization. Today, only four market-rate units are available despite premium rents (3–7 percent premiums for one-bedroom and studio units, more than a 25 percent premium for two- and three-bedroom units) for East Harlem. Tapestry stands as an example of how affordable workforce housing can make a significant contribution to the culture and character of a historic urban neighborhood.

Lessons from Industry Leaders

Jonathan Rose, President
Jonathan Rose Companies
New York, New York

RICHARD ROSAN: You partnered with a local construction company to create this project. Can you explain how Tapestry began?

JONATHAN ROSE: We do a lot of work in Harlem. We were looking for more projects in the area when Lettire Construction came to us with an interesting site. They owned some parcels that were interlaced with city parcels in a way that neither Lettire nor the city could do much without the help of the other. The city was interested in developing affordable housing on the site, and Lettire was interested in developing market-rate housing. Lettire hadn't done a project this large so they came to us.

ROSAN: It was a complex partnership, correct?

ROSE: It was. One of the first things Lettire had to prove to the city was that by doing a joint development with the Jonathan Rose Companies, they could create more affordable housing than if they just built affordable housing on the small parcels they owned. The second issue was the site was being rezoned through the city's River to River Rezoning initiative. Our designers—Harry Cobb as a coarchitect along with a wonderful affordable housing architect named Herbert Mandel—came up with a beautiful building concept that took the premise of the future proposed zoning into account. So we worked with the city planning department on our plan, which was a mixed-income project that included retail on the ground floor.

ROSAN: How closely did you work with the city?

ROSE: The city planning department was very supportive of the project because it reflected the goals of this new zoning, which was contentious in Harlem at the time. They could point to our project and say, "When the zoning passes, this project will get approved and this is the type of project that will be built in the future." That got the support of the community board, which wanted a balance of affordable and market-rate housing in the neighborhood as a sustainable model going forward.

ROSAN: Could you go into more detail about the River to River Rezoning Plan?

ROSE: In many ways, the zoning shaped the building. The proposed zoning had a 120-foot height limit so we were restricted there: we could only build 12 stories. On the other hand, at that height we could use block-and-plank construction, which in New York City is much less expensive then concrete frame construction—around 30 to 40 percent cheaper than the alternative. And because our partner was also our contractor, we were able to build a beautiful and very sustainable building for what is a very affordable price—for New York at least.

ROSAN: How was the land acquired?

ROSE: We bought some of the land and then we received city-donated land, so our total land cost was very very low—under $20 per square foot.

ROSAN: How about construction costs?

ROSE: The construction cost was $20 per square foot, which in New York is extremely low. We used nonunion construction but at living wages, which was facilitated by our partner Lettire.

ROSAN: And the city allows you to do that?

ROSE: New York is very good not only at setting high affordable housing goals but also at helping developers achieve those goals. Mayor Bloomberg has set a goal of 165,000 affordable units and has really allocated a lot of money and resources toward that effort. The city recognizes that if you build affordable housing at the prevailing wage, there would be 25 percent fewer units. And when you are looking at a goal of 165,000, that is 30,000 or 40,000 fewer units because of higher labor costs. So the city leaves it up to the developer to handle labor costs, and instead focuses on the funding side.

ROSAN: How about financing?

ROSE: We were able to get 4 percent Low-Income Housing Tax Credits on the affordable units, which we sold to PNC Bank and then the city also brought in other subsidies—basically gap fillers. Altogether, the two partners put in $14 million in equity on a $70 million project.

ROSAN: Let's just diverge for a minute on the sustainable elements—what are they?

ROSE: Tapestry's location is its most important green feature. It's a transit-oriented development, walkable to subway and commuter lines, near a supermarket and the commercial corridor of Harlem. The second most important element is woven into the architecture: we created all these large bay windows—it actually looks like a very contemporary version of a 1920s building—that create a lot of cross ventilation and daylighting that boost its

energy efficiency while also adding to its aesthetic presence.

ROSAN: Were there any challenges developing a green building?

ROSE: Since we had HUD [Department of Housing and Urban Development] funding we had to do a noise study. Since we are close to the RFK Bridge, it required that most of the windows be triple glazed, which is good for bringing in daylight but not so good for drawing in heat. Another drawback was we could not use in-window air conditioners because of the high noise. It's an example of a cost burden when building workforce and affordable housing under HUD regulations.

ROSAN: What is your philosophy on sustainable design?

ROSE: We are very interested not only in developing buildings that by their nature are green but in shifting the behavior of people in the building so as to be greener. What we have learned actually through something called the Garrison Institute Climate, Mind and Behavior program is that people can reduce energy costs by about 30 percent through behavior change. For example, turning off the lights when you leave the apartment or educating staff on energy efficiency—it's a very simple thing. We are running an interesting experiment: About half our units come with electric outlets that have an IP address on each one. Using an iPhone, computer, or smartphone, you can control and monitor the usage of every outlet.

ROSAN: How does that work?

ROSE: A modern TV, for instance, uses more electricity when it's off than a refrigerator does. So does your cable box. These smart outlets give people the ability to turn those things off or to program them—if you want to come home and watch the news at 6:00, you can have your TV turn on at 5:45. So we are giving residents real-time data through these outlets and real-time control, and the experiment is to see how much a green apartment saves versus an apartment that is green but also gives the resident feedback and control. We are doing this with Columbia's Center for Research and Environmental Decisions.

ROSAN: What does the resident profile of Tapestry look like?

ROSE: It's amazing because the income mix ranges from about $16,000 a year to $400,000 a year. One very important lesson we have learned is that income mixing is actually very easy. I give a lot of lectures on affordable housing, and this is the question I'm always asked: "Will rich people and poor people live together?" The answer is that people don't necessarily select by income or class. These are mostly working people, and just look at the way people dress today, you really can't tell who makes more than the other.

ROSAN: And how did the lease-up go?

ROSE: It's been interesting. No surprise on the low-income housing component: there is a huge waiting list; it's 100 percent full. The moderate-income housing had a longer lease-up period but is now 100 percent full and has no turnover. The reason it took longer to lease is that people earning $60,000 to $90,000 a year are not used to dealing with these government processes. They come in and don't realize that you need to be income certified. So instead of

filling out these forms and waiting, they'll say, "Well, I can go rent an apartment in Queens," which is true. But they can't rent an apartment as nice as this in this location. So it took longer to fill, but these residents are not moving. It is extremely stable.

ROSAN: What about the market-rate units?

ROSE: In essence, half the building is subsidized, has lower rents, and has zero vacancy. The other half of the building has both the upside and downside of market risk, and the market dropped.

ROSAN: What is the market rate?

ROSE: We are now renting about $40 per square foot. So, for example, a market-rate studio is about $1,800 a month; a one-bedroom is $2,260; a two-bedroom is $3,000 or about $3,100; and a three-bedroom is about $3,600. But that is still well below something that would be on the east side of Manhattan, some 30 or 40 blocks north.